W9-AZL-890

Christmas in Wales

BY JANE MAAS

Adventures of an Advertising Woman

Better Brochures, Catalogs and Mailing Pieces

How to Advertise (with Ken Roman)

The New How to Advertise (with Ken Roman)

Christmas in Wales

A HOMECOMING

Jane & Michael Maas

St. Martin's Press

NEW YORK

PERMISSIONS

From *Finnegans Wake* by James Joyce. Copyright 1939 by James Joyce, Copyright renewed © 1967 by Giorgio Joyce and Lucia Joyce. Used by permission of Viking Penguin, a division of Penguin Books USA Inc.

Dylan Thomas: *A Child's Christmas in Wales.* Copyright © 1952 by Dylan Thomas. Reprinted by permission of New Directions Publishing Corp.

Dylan Thomas: *Poems of Dylan Thomas.* Copyright 1945 by The Trustees for the Copyrights of Dylan Thomas, 1952 by Dylan Thomas. Reprinted by permission of New Directions Publishing Corp.

Reprinted with permission of Macmillan Publishing Company from *The Poems of W. B. Yeats: A New Edition,* edited by Richard J. Finneran (New York: Macmillan, 1983).

CHRISTMAS IN WALES: A HOMECOMING
Copyright © 1994 by Jane and Michael Maas. All rights reserved. Printed in the United States of America. No part of this book may be used or reproduced in any manner whatsoever without written permission except in the case of brief quotations embodied in critical articles or reviews. For information, address St. Martin's Press, 175 Fifth Avenue, New York, N.Y. 10010.

Production Editor: David Stanford Burr
Designer: Sara Stemen

LIBRARY OF CONGRESS CATALOGING-IN-PUBLICATION DATA
Maas, Jane
    Christmas in Wales / Jane and Michael Maas.
        p.   cm.
    "A Thomas Dunne book."
    ISBN 0-312-11464-8
    1. Christmas—Wales.   2. Thomas family.   3. Lloyd
family.   4. Wales—Social life and customs.   5. Wales—
Genealogy.   I. Maas, Michael, 1951- . II. Title.
GT4987.465.M33   1994
394.2' 663' 09429—dc20   94-22536
                                                                                    CIP

First Edition: November 1994

10 9 8 7 6 5 4 3 2 1

This book is for Kate and Jenny.
And in loving memory of the
two beautiful Welsh sisters,
Mary and Margaret.

Acknowledgments

The authors wish to thank Gail and David Lloyd, Nona Rees, all the other celebrants in the eisteddfod at Felin Isaf, and the people of St. David's who welcomed us home for Christmas.

We are grateful to Tom Dunne and Pete Wolverton at St. Martin's Press; Julian Bach, our literary agent; and Bob Evans for much-needed advice on Welsh grammar and spelling. Thanks also to Jeb Brown and the staff of the Westhampton Free Library, on whose computers we wrote this book.

And special thanks to Dr. Ken Leiby of New Hope for sharing his memories.

Contents

Christmas in Wales

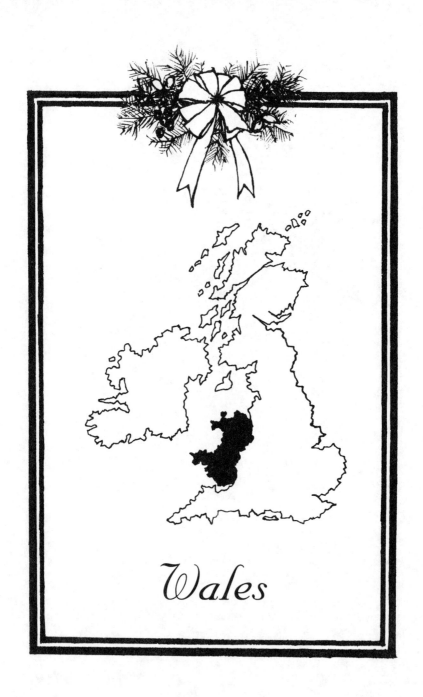

Wales

The Christmas Angel

Jane Writes

It was raining that June morning as we came into the Presbyterian chapel in New Hope, Pennsylvania, for Aunt Mary's funeral. Mim was my mother's identical twin and my own surrogate mother. Although she had never visited Wales, Mim was the fiercest Welsh nationalist of all our large clan of Thomases and Lloyds. This service was only for the family, but we almost filled the chapel—Mim's husband, her children and grandchildren, brother, nieces and nephews, grandnieces and grandnephews.

The organist played "The Little Brown Church in the Vale," then the minister spoke. "I am the resurrection, and the life," he began, and the words comforted me as they had at my mother's funeral almost exactly twenty years before.

Uncle Ken had asked their sons, Dan and Mike, to read something Mim would have liked. Dan chose Dylan Thomas's "Do Not Go Gentle into

That Good Night." He changed the word *father* in one line to *mother*, and his voice quavered as he spoke it.

And you, my [mother], there on the sad height,
Curse, bless, me now with your fierce tears, I pray.
Do not go gentle into that good night.

Mike read the closing paragraphs of *How Green Was My Valley*, with its lament for the dead and reaffirmation of life. Uncle Ken had asked me to say a few words, too. "You're the one in the family who inherited her way with words. Give her a good Welsh send-off."

As I stood up, the rain stopped and the sun came out. "Well, Mim," I said, "obviously that's you, giving out marching orders again. We knew you wouldn't let it rain on your parade." The congregation chuckled. Most of us had been on the receiving end of Mim's famous marching orders at some point during our childhoods.

I spoke briefly, simply celebrating what Mim had meant to me. I loved my gentle, self-effacing mother, but I adored Mim and wanted to be just like her. "I'm Welsh, black Welsh," she told me over and over. "And you're half Welsh—the *best* half of you."

Welshmen traditionally wear a leek in their hats on March 1, the birthday of St. David, patron saint of Wales. Mim wore her leek jauntily every year. She was visiting our home in Union City, New Jersey, one St. David's Day when I was six or seven. I noticed the leek, investigated more closely, wrinkled my nose, and objected that it smelled like an onion. Mim tapped my chest with the busy forefinger she used for emphasis. "That is the national symbol of Wales, miss. It does indeed smell like an onion. A good honest smell, like Welsh earth."

So I wore a leek in my hat on St. David's Day for a few years, until I became an adolescent and was embarrassed to seem different. Later, as an advertising copywriter in my first agency job, I started wearing it again, enjoying the eccentricity. After I married Michael, a conservative architect, I stopped wearing the leek because it embarrassed *him*.

Michael and I drove frequently from New York City to New Hope to visit Mim and Uncle Ken during her illness. The last time I saw her, she looked slim and young and, even with her white hair, very much like the aunt I remembered.

She was sitting up in the canopied bed, wearing a frilly white bed jacket and smoking a cigarette. A few minutes later, she noted that it was almost time for lunch. Uncle Ken, wanting to keep up her strength, asked if she would like a chocolate ice cream soda.

"I would like a gin martini, very dry," Mim said. "Michael, you make superb martinis. Will you do the honors?" Michael opened his mouth to protest, but Mim pointed an imperious forefinger at him.

"With a twist." Michael and Uncle Ken went meek-
ly down to the kitchen.

We had a few minutes alone, and we were candid
with each other, as we always had been. "What am I
going to do without you?" I asked her.

"Just remember me," she said. "And don't forget
that leek."

"I won't," I promised. "Ever." Mim died the next
day.

The organ played the Welsh anthem "Men of
Harlech" as we left the chapel and went down the
path to the old cemetery. Uncle Ken gave each one
of us a flower to place on her grave. "They're from
her garden," he said, and for the first time since the
day began, his eyes were wet behind his familiar
square glasses.

Fittingly, it began to rain again.

I spent a few days in New Hope to help my
cousins sort out Mim's things. We all wanted to
spare Uncle Ken any difficult moments, but he was
with me in the storeroom on the third floor when
we found the Christmas ornaments.

There were boxes and boxes of them. "Oh my,"
Uncle Ken said quietly. "You take any of these that
you want, Jane. I don't believe I'll be putting up a
Christmas tree around here anymore." He left me
alone in the big cedar-scented room.

As an adult, I always gave Mim tree ornaments as
Christmas gifts, and I recognized some of them
now: sharp-edged tin animals we bought for her in
Mexico; a straw doll from Tuscany; a papier-mâché
cactus from New Mexico.

Inside another box, wrapped in tissue, were dozens of fragile balls with Christmas scenes painted on them. They looked familiar, but I couldn't fix the memory. I picked up a larger, heavier object, wrapped even more carefully. The tissue came away and there she was. She had lost most of her nose and her blue robe was faded, but I remembered her vividly. She was the angel who had always stood at the top of the tree all the Christmases of my childhood, the Welsh Christmases in the coal regions of Pennsylvania.

There was a note in the bottom of the box, and I recognized Mim's handwriting. She was constantly making lists, writing in a diary or jotting notes to herself. That's what this one was.

"New Year's Eve, 1985. We took the tree down early this year. A good Christmas, but *next* Christmas, as God is my witness, I am going to Wales. To see if there are any of our Lloyd and Thomas family still there. And to hear Welsh singing in a Welsh valley once before I die."

I knew she hadn't made it to Wales, and knew, just as certainly, that I would make the journey for her. "You've given me my marching orders, Mim," I said. "Christmas in Wales."

I wrapped the angel back in tissue paper and took her downstairs.

CHAPTER ONE

Christmases in the Pennsylvania Coal Regions

Jane Writes

My mother's family, Lloyds and Thomases, emigrated from Wales to the United States in the 1840s. They had been coal miners in Wales, so they became coal miners in Pennsylvania, settling in the little town of Shamokin, sixty miles southwest of Scranton. By the time I was born in 1932, in the midst of the Depression, they had risen out of the mines but not out of their Welshness. And no celebrations were more Welsh than Christmas.

My grandmother was the matriarch of the family. She and Grandad lived in Lewisburg, Pennsylvania, where they ran the Maymar Tea Room, named for their twin daughters, my mother, Margaret, and her sister, Mary. After Grandad died, when I was a baby, Gran ran the tearoom alone. The restaurant was popular among the faculty members at Bucknell University because the food was good and the prices were right. Beef stew was forty cents and a

slice of Gran's apple pie *with* home-
made vanilla ice cream was ten. The
food was hearty. The Bucknell football
team had their training table there in
season, and Gran could turn out twenty
pies at a clip in her scary black coal-
burning stove, which was never allowed
to go out.

The few women who taught at Bucknell, in what was still known as the
Women's Seminary, liked to eat at the
tearoom because Gran was almost one
of their own, a former elementary
schoolteacher. Even more important to them, she
was a no-nonsense Presbyterian. They knew she
would never allow anything stronger than tea in her
teacups. Even after Prohibition was repealed, Gran
led the charge to keep Lewisburg dry. She suc-
ceeded almost too well in this mission; when I grad-
uated from Bucknell University in 1953, the
strongest drink available in Lewisburg was the 2.5
percent beer sold at the Hotel Lewisburger on Mar-
ket Street.

Every Christmas, my mother and father and I
traveled from home in Union City to Lewisburg.
By the time I was six and seven and eight, the trip—
and all of Christmas—began to take on the rituals
of myth. It was always a long, cold trip, at least six
hours in our unheated Chevrolet, where I sat in the
backseat with a blanket. We would drive past
Secaucus, New Jersey, which smelled of pig farms,

and past Jersey City, which was perfumed with sulfur from the chemical plants. "What is that smell?" I asked once, and my mother said snippily, "New Jersey." She never quite forgave my father for taking her away from Pennsylvania.

Dad tried to keep me entertained by looking for exotic out-of-state licenses and, as we reached more rural areas, various breeds of cows—holsteins, Guernseys, and Jerseys. For a city child, cows were a curiosity, and looking for them kept me occupied for hours.

We crossed the Delaware at Easton, then drove through Bethlehem, where we stopped to admire the crèche in the center of town. "This year's is the prettiest crèche they've ever had," we agreed annually, in ritual response. I always knew we were getting near Gran's house when it got dark and the Christmas lights came on in the towns where my mother grew up: Tamaqua, Mahanoy City, Shamokin, and, finally, Lewisburg.

Because we had the longest journey to make, we were always the last of the family to arrive. Gran always came out to the car, hugging herself in the cold, kissed my mother, greeted my father formally, and carried me into the house. She was short and plump and wore her gray hair pulled straight back into a bun underneath a hair net secured with big dark brown hairpins. Her dresses, in soft widow's colors of lilac or beige, had short sleeves so she could plunge her hands deep into a bowl of dough without having to bother about rolling them up.

Gran always smelled of pie crusts and talcum powder.

She seemed old to me, as grandparents usually do, but I think now she was only in her middle forties. At only twenty, she had married my grandfather, who was twenty years her senior. My great-great-aunt Jenny—Jane Lloyd, after whom I was named—was in her late seventies. She sat in a rocking chair most of the time and dozed.

Great-Aunt Lib, Gran's younger sister, had been the beauty of the family. She was the giddy one, the flirt, the actress. She was giddier than ever at Christmas, due to excitement and eggnog, and people constantly said to her, gently reproving, "Oh, *Libby!*" Her husband, Bill, much in demand by the little boys, was warden of the Pottsville jail! Some Christmases, Uncle Bill brought with him a trustee named Jack to help Gran with the extra chores of the holidays. Jack was a mild-looking man who wore a nondescript gray uniform, not prison stripes at all. But we cousins whispered to one another that he had killed a man! Poor Jack. We dogged his footsteps and gave him no peace.

Great-Uncle Garfield Thomas was Gran's older brother. He had a large stomach, a red nose, and looked a lot like W. C. Fields. His wife, Great-Aunt Emmaline, was tall and spare. The handsomest uncle of all was mother's younger brother, Bill, who wrestled on the Bucknell team and did mock exhibitions for us kids.

It was Mim who made Christmas magical for us. Her husband, Dan, was a navy lieutenant, away at sea much of the time, so Mim was the only adult who didn't have a spouse to be responsible for.* She could devote all her time to us. When it snowed, she took us sleigh riding on the Bucknell campus and helped roll the big ball for the body of the snowman.

She took us to Bechtel's Dairy Store for ice cream cones when most grown-ups we knew thought ice cream was taboo on frigid days. Mim believed it warmed you up. She let us have double dips and pile on the brown sprinkles we called "worms."

She taught us to sing a Welsh children's song about buying a broom from a broomstick man. I can only reproduce it phonetically.

> *Gwella king ah, key burnee skeebit,*
> *Burnee skeebit, burnee skeebit.*
> *Gwella king ah, key burnee skeebit,*
> *Burnee skeebit, gwenee.*

We loved her mystical powers over animals and inanimate objects. Dogs were mesmerized by Mim, who gave them snappy naval commands. "Sit down, sir!" she would order, and the dog, male or female, pet or stray, would sink to the floor in ecstacy, haunches quivering.

Some evenings, Mim and my mother would "tip

---

*Uncle Dan was killed in the Pacific during World War II. Mim later married Bucks County's much-loved physician, Dr. Ken Leiby.

the table" and communicate with the spirit world. They placed their hands, fingers touching, lightly on a table and—even if it was a big heavy one—the table would *tip*!

Mim was always the spokesman and translator. "Is anyone there?" she would ask. "Is anyone there? Tip the table, please." It was the same commanding voice she used with dogs, and even spirits had to obey. One tap was for yes and two for no; one tap for *A,* two for *B,* and so on. We cousins sat in the darkened room and listened as Mim deciphered the messages.

You could never tell who your ghostly communicator might be. We had sessions with Julius Caesar and George Washington. Once the spirit identified itself by tapping out E-L-I-Z-A-B-E-T-H. "Elizabeth?" Mary asked. "Are you *Queen* Elizabeth?" The table raised itself high and gave one loud, disdainful rap.

One night, we were contacted by Uncle Lloyd. "But, Uncle Lloyd," Mim objected, "you are in Harrisburg." It turned out Uncle Lloyd was not, indeed, in Harrisburg. He had died late that very afternoon.

When I was older, I asked Mim what the trick was. She looked at me with astonishment. "Why, Jane, there is no trick. You just have to be Welsh and believe in it."

Finally, each year, it was Christmas Eve. On this day, everybody was assigned a job. The children helped decorate the tree. The strings of lights had to

be twined around the tree before the decorations
went on, and they had to be tested, one by one, by
the uncles. If even a single bulb was dead, the entire
string would fail. We children cheered when the
lights blinked on. Then we worked on the annual
homemade ornaments: garlands of colored con-
struction-paper loops glued together with library
paste; garlands of popcorn and cranberries skew-
ered on Gran's biggest darning needles, until our
fingers were sticky with cranberry juice and the
floor was dusty with popcorn bits. Mim's dog, a
white chow named Vixen, in the first of her holiday
feasting, scavenged popcorn droppings.

The ornaments went on next. Then Aunt Emmaline came and supervised the placement of the tinsel, strand by strand. This part always bored the
uncles. They wanted to throw the tinsel in handfuls
at the tree and let it land willy-nilly. Only Em had
the patience for this part. I remember she *un-
trimmed* the tinsel, too, and folded it away, strand
by strand, in tissue. The family teased her about
that, since tinsel was so cheap and disposable.
When the war broke out and there was no more
foil, Aunt Em was vindicated. For all the war years,
our tree was the only one in Lewisburg trimmed
with tinsel.

The next-to-last touch was a white material
called "angel's hair," which looked like spun cotton
candy. It was intended to make the Christmas tree
appear ethereal and snowy, but it was made of
fiberglass, so there was a sting beneath its soft sur-

face. We trimmers itched miserably all through Christmas.

Finally, it was time to place the angel at the top of the tree. Gran told us that her own parents had brought the angel with them from Wales. She was an old-fashioned Victorian figure with a sweet childish face, blond hair, and a sky blue robe. The whole family had to stop whatever they were doing and watch this ceremony. Young Uncle Bill, the most agile of the men, climbed a little stepladder to fasten her to the pinnacle. The aunts would call directions. "A little to the left, Bill." "A little higher." When the angel was enthroned, the tree was finished.

Then it was time to bake gingerbread men. Gran had been baking other kinds of cookies for weeks and had whipped up dozens of different kinds. There were butter cookies in shapes you could play with before you ate them; Christmas trees with green sprinkles; bells with red sprinkles; tin soldiers with tiny silver candies for buttons; hearts and diamonds and spades dusted with cinnamon and sugar; and drop cookies, some made with oatmeal, others stuffed with raisins and candied fruit or crunchy with cornflakes and shredded coconut. We especially liked snickerdoodles, for the name more than the taste. These were Pennsylvania Dutch cookies made with currants and walnuts. In a separate class, off limits to us, were the company cookies, which were baked for grown-ups: white meringue cookies, chocolate lace cookies, macaroons, almond crescents. Cookies were everywhere in Gran's house: in cookie jars and Mason jars, on platters and raised stands and three-tiered lazy Susans painted with reindeer.

Oh, Christmas Eve was full of rituals! There was the eating of the first gingerbread men. Did you bite the head off first, or a leg, or just an ear? Vixen didn't particularly like gingerbread, but she always tasted a few body parts just to make sure. By late afternoon, Gran stuffed the turkey. There were always two kinds of stuffing: bread stuffing (the bread had to be two-days *stale*) for the main cavity and chestnut stuffing for the neck. The turkey, a twenty-five-pound giant, went into the black oven to roast slowly all night long.

By late afternoon, the uncles made their famous fishhouse punch, the most popular holiday drink in Lewisburg. Gran's house was always full of friends and neighbors on Christmas Eve, drinking punch and nibbling cookies. One year, because I was the oldest of the cousins, my uncles let me in on a secret and made me promise not to tell a soul. They had laced the punch with rum.

Lots of fruit juices and ginger ale went into fishhouse punch, and it tasted so wholesome that it fooled even the teetotaling members of the Presbyterian Ladies Aid Society. The uncles told that

story every Christmas afterward and it entered into
legend: the year the Presbyterian ladies all got tipsy.

Usually, the ladies had one polite cup of punch
and nibbled a cookie while their husbands gathered
in the kitchen with the uncles for something a little
stronger. After about twenty minutes, the ladies
normally fetched their husbands, kissed the aunts,
shook hands with the uncles, and continued their
holiday calls.

That year, however, the fishhouse punch stopped
them in their tracks. Uncle Garf officiated at the
punch bowl and offered seconds. "Why, Garfield,
this punch is delicious," the minister's wife re-
marked as she raised her empty punch cup in a
fawn-gloved hand. "And so pretty with the straw-
berries floating in it. I believe I will." And all the
other ladies said why, yes, they believed they would
have a second cup, too. Uncle Garf ladled and
Uncle Bill and my father made another batch of
punch in the kitchen.

Later on, I noticed that some of the Presbyterian
ladies were laughing very loudly. They were gathered around my handsome uncle Bill, who was
showing them wrestling holds! One of the ladies
began to hiccup, and Uncle Garf tried to frighten
her into stopping but couldn't, which caused more
laughter. The minister's wife, however, was crying
and blowing her nose and talking about Christmases gone by.

The minister put an end to the festivities. He
took his wife by the arm. "Come along, Edna," he

said stiffly. "You are having a crying jag." And the next day, we learned that the Presbyterian ladies didn't continue on their usual round of polite holiday calls. They all went home to bed.

Did we never eat dinner on Christmas Eve? I don't think so, not ever. The grown-ups were busy with their guests, and Gran was preoccupied with next day's feast. We children were so stuffed with cookies and cocoa that we couldn't, at that moment, eat a morsel. As I look back, it is odd that in that household of nurturing women not once did one say, "Good heavens, the children haven't had a bite to eat for dinner!"

As soon as it was dark, we turned on the Christmas tree lights. Then, no matter how bitterly cold it was, the carolers came and we opened the front door to listen, to show them we appreciated their singing. They sang the old favorites. "O Come, All Ye Faithful," "Good King Wenceslas," "It Came Upon the Midnight Clear," "Deck the Halls," and, as the finale, "Silent Night." Sometimes the carolers came in for punch and cookies; most years, they passed the hat and went on their way.

At bedtime, the cousins went to the bedroom we shared, willing the night to be over fast so Christmas morning would be here. My cousins usually fell asleep quickly, but I tossed, listening to the rumbling voices of the uncles, fortified by punch, downstairs. Sometimes, I woke in the middle of the night and didn't know where I was until I smelled Gran's turkey and the Christmas tree and heard my cousins breathing and Vixen, who had overeaten, moaning softly in the darkness.

On Christmas morning, the family gathered in the living room, in pajamas and bathrobes, and opened presents. There was no designated Santa Claus, no master of ceremonies, no orderly opening of gift and thanking of giver one by one. No, this was a kind of melee, with every man for himself. Some of the gifts were expected every year. Gran knit us each something warm and practical; Aunt Lib gave us something silly and unsubstantial and sure to be broken by evening. Usually, Mother and Aunt Mary presented each other identical gifts, not by design but because, as twins, they thought the same way. Vixen always got a new dog dish, which she ignored, and a big Christmas bow, which she hated.

Mim always gave me a book, and it was almost always a book about heroes. She introduced me to *Robin Hood, The White Company, Ivanhoe, Ben Hur,* and, when she thought I was ready, Malory's *Morte d'Arthur.*

Aunt Em gathered up the discarded ribbons and bows, smoothed out any wrapping paper that had not been ripped to pieces, and put them all away for next year. It was a signal that one part of Christmas was over.

Christmas dinner never varied: the turkey and its stuffings; giblet gravy; little onions in cream sauce; a whole cauliflower surrounded by a rim of green peas; two varieties of cranberry sauce, one jellied and one whole; mashed potatoes, whipped into whorls with hot milk and butter; and one vegetable the children didn't like, mashed turnips, with their peppery taste and rooty undertaste.

Gran presided at the head of the table because she carved better than any of the uncles. My father always asked for, and received, "the part that goes over the fence last," and Gran dispensed drumsticks to children who were old enough to finish them. Younger children were awarded wings; the very young had to be content with white meat. Then side dishes were passed. Someone had to go to the kitchen and refill the gravy boat. And finally, as the food on our plates cooled, Gran called on Uncle Garf to say grace. It was fitting for her to cook and even to carve, but in a Welsh family it was a man who invoked the Almighty. And then, at last, we ate.

Dessert was a parade of pies—apple, mince, and pecan—and Aunt Lib's plum pudding, which she had been dousing with brandy for months. The grown-ups had coffee, and the uncles put a dollop of rum in theirs. So did Aunt Lib, because, as she said, it was only once a year.

After dinner, it was time for a Welsh celebration. Everyone present was expected to entertain, usually by reciting poetry. My mother and Mim performed together, the prerogative of twins. Usually, they enacted a scene from Shakespeare. My father went next, to get it over with, and generally read "Gunga Din." Young Uncle Bill, not to be outdone, countered with "Casey at the Bat." Then Uncle Garf, who was a romantic, always stood up with a volume of Yeats in his hands and read to Aunt Em.

When you are old and grey and full of sleep,
And nodding by the fire, take down this book,
And slowly read, and dream of the soft look
Your eyes had once, and of their shadows deep...

Then, at last, it was time for Aunt Lib, the poetry-reciting champion of the coal regions. She would stand and announce the title gravely. The children's favorite was Poe's "The Raven," which Lib performed from memory, complete with hoarse croaks and flapping of wings. Sometimes she did "Curfew Must Not Ring Tonight," "Horatius at the Bridge," or "The Charge of the Light Brigade." Aunt Lib recited on other family occasions, but she was never more dramatic than after her tot of rum at Christmas.

Such were the Welsh Christmases in the coal regions of Pennsylvania. I wondered whether

Christmas in Wales would be not only a journey made as a promise to Mim but a trip back for me to that mythic time of my childhood.

CHAPTER TWO

Preparations

Michael Writes

Mim had been one of my favorites among Jane's Welsh clan. When Jane told me about finding her note and wanting to spend the following Christmas in Wales, I was all for it. I did think, however, that it was unlikely we would find any trace of the Thomas and Lloyd families after all these years.

Strange that in the thirty-five years of our marriage we had never visited Wales. We'd been to England a dozen times, to France almost every October, to Italy and Spain and Greece and Japan. As an architect, I'd written articles about Paris, London, and Florence. But we'd never even considered a trip to Wales. Was Jane afraid that it would disappoint her?

Now the question was, Where in Wales should we spend Christmas and hunt for those long-lost cousins? The trail had grown cold. Margaret and Mary were gone. The only Welsh uncle left was

Bill, the college wrestler, who said he remembered vaguely that the family came from Carmarthenshire, in the southwest.

After some reading about that area, we chose St. David's as home base. Birthplace of the patron saint of Wales, it is officially a city—the smallest one in Britain—because it has a cathedral. Without the cathedral, St. David's would be just a little town of seventeen hundred people.

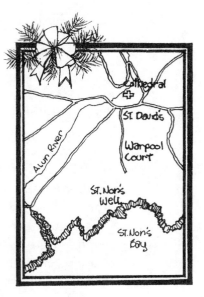

Jane said that where there was a cathedral, there should be a library. She dug into the subject and by early autumn struck up a correspondence with Nona Rees, librarian of the cathedral and of the city, as well. My wife, who headed an advertising agency, is an accomplished researcher. She spends six months preparing for every trip we take and always comes up with astounding discoveries. Finding Nona was her all-time best.

First, Nona knew everybody in St. David's and the surrounding country. She told us that it wouldn't be very hard to find Thomases and Lloyds, since they were the most common family names in the area. The trick would be in finding the *right* Thomases and Lloyds. Nona signed on for the hunt with enthusiasm, writing us, "This is going to be *fun!*"

Nona is also an historian, author of a book on the life of St. David, and an antiquarian with special knowledge of pre-Christian history. We gave her the long list of things we wanted to do and places we wanted to explore during our week in Wales: architecture, castles, St. David's Cathedral, churches, Celtic crosses, standing stones, sites associated with Druids, saints, King Arthur, seacoast walks. Nona said she would be delighted to be our guide.

She ended her first letter to us with this postscript: "Just to warn you that Christmas Eve is one of my ridiculously busy days. A small group of us (quite insanely when there is so much work to do) go carol singing round the city. We are all—or have been—cathedral choristers and so sing the carols in four-part harmony. It's great fun and if all goes well I hope you'll be able to have a listen."

Where would we stay? Nona suggested St. Non's Hotel. (St. Non was the mother of St. David. She gave birth to him just outside the city, on a cliff overlooking the bay.) It was the only hotel in the city, she believed, that would be open during Christmas. They would make us warm and welcome. "Speaking of warmth," Nona added, "let me warn you that Wales is usually wet and cold in December. Bring warm waterproof coats and—most important—good stout boots."

We made our plane reservations. To London on December twenty-second, to Wales on December twenty-third. Jane called St. Non's Hotel; they could give us a room for that entire week. The first night was only twenty-five pounds per person for bed and breakfast, inexpensive for Britain. (The pound was then worth about $1.50.)

"Twenty-five pounds for bed and breakfast?" Jane repeated happily. I chuckled to myself as I listened to her. My wife is a miserly soul who loves a bargain, especially when it comes to vacations. "That's terrific!"

Then her tone changed. "Two hundred and ten pounds per person for three days?" she asked in horror. The hotel explained that this was a special rate for Christmas Eve, Christmas Day, and Boxing Day and that it included not only bed and breakfast but tea and dinner, as well.

"How come it's so much higher than the usual rate?" Jane persisted.

The answer was simple: Because it was Christmas.

I knew from Jane's expression that she was about to turn them down and begin a hunt for something less expensive. "It's only once a year," I urged. "Maybe once in a lifetime. Make the reservation."

We would stay at St. Non's.

By November, Nona was writing at least every week with suggestions for adven-

tures and day trips: Pembroke Castle; St. Non's
Well; the Celtic cross at Nevern, one of the finest in
Wales; the great cromlech, a pre-Christian burial
mound, at Pentre Ifan. St. David's Cathedral, of
course, was her special subject. Did we want to
spend a day in Carmarthen seeing the birthplace of
Merlin? Or Laugharne, where Dylan Thomas once
lived?

Every time Nona wrote, Jane telephoned in
reply. As Christmas approached, the letters and
calls accelerated. One day, AT&T contacted us to
offer a preferred rate to Britain. We had called there
so often in the past two months, they said, we obviously had relatives there. "Yes and no," I replied.

Only two weeks to go. "I have a find for you,"
Nona wrote us excitedly. "A couple named Lloyd,
David and Gail Lloyd, who also have Thomases in
their family tree. They live in a medieval mill in St.
David's. They've remodeled it and take some visi-
tors on a bed-and-breakfast basis. And although it
is Christmas and a family time, they just might put
you up for a night or two."

Jane immediately called the Lloyds and found
David at home. He was skeptical and a bit gruff, she
told me later. Christmas was the busiest time of
year for his wife; children coming home. Hmpf.
Call back later in the day and speak to Gail.

Gail Lloyd said it was quite possible, as long as
we waited until Christmas was over. She and Jane
agreed on the mill for bed and breakfast our last
two nights in Wales. Gail invited us and Nona to

share a traditional Welsh dinner. We thanked her
and said we would bring the wine.

A last letter came from Nona, reporting another
find. On the Sunday after Christmas, a Welsh geologist would conduct a walking tour in the Preseli
Hills. We could visit Iron Age forts and the site
where, according to legend, the famous bluestones
of Stonehenge had been quarried. Nona planned to
go herself; wouldn't we come along? Jane telephoned and, with a sense of enormous urgency,
asked Nona to reserve our places for the walk
before they were all snapped up. Nona chortled
that a December walk in the mountains would
hardly attract an army. She mentioned stout boots
again and said she would see us in a week at the
Haverfordwest train station.

We began prepacking in order to figure out how
many suitcases we would eventually need. We decided on long johns, mittens, and wool caps for the
coast walks, slightly dressy clothing for Christmas
Day, and slacks and sweaters, books, guidebooks,
and binoculars. I surveyed the mound—a veritable
cromlech.

It was time to buy that warm waterproof outer-
wear, which we, as New Yorkers, didn't own. Jane
found a duck hunter's jacket, all zippers and pock-
ets and Velcro fasteners. She disappeared into it as if
into a tent, but she looked cute, so we bought it. I
ordered a sturdy coat from the J. Crew catalog.

The waterproof shoes were harder to find. Jane
wanted comfort and old-fashioned Wellingtons. I

bought a pair of good-looking rubber-soled moccasins. They weren't particularly warm or waterproof, but I didn't expect we'd be splashing around
in much cold water. Skeptical, Jane bought a matching pair. They went onto the mound.

The confirmation arrived from St. Non's Hotel,
along with a printed message. "Gentlemen are
invited to wear dinner jackets for the Boxing Day
dinner dance." Time was too short for an exchange
of letters, so Jane telephoned to ask, "What does it
mean that gentlemen are 'invited' to wear dinner
jackets?"

"Well, dear, most gentlemen *do*," she was told.
My dinner jacket and Jane's cocktail dress joined
the growing mound and I added a third suitcase,
more than we had ever traveled with before.

Jane made one last call to the Lloyds to confirm
dates, then reported the conversation. Gail said she
had invited her sister, who is a student of family
trees, to our special dinner. David Lloyd got on the
telephone to ask when Jane's family left Wales for
the United States. "In the 1840s," she told him.

"That's when my family left, too," he acknowl-
edged. "But that's not a coincidence. *Everybody* left
about then because there was a famine."

"I thought the famine was in Ireland," Jane said.

"Well, it was in Wales, too," David answered.
"Where did your family settle?"

"In Pennsylvania—Shamokin, Pennsylvania."

"Well, God knows where mine went," David
said. "I think some of them went to Patagonia.

Don't get your hopes up. It's a needle in a haystack."

My coat arrived from J. Crew and Jane sulked slightly. It looked much more elegant than her duck hunter's tent. I put in a last-minute call to J. Crew and ordered a superrush overnight delivery of an extrasmall version of my coat.

Only two days to go. We had a family gathering to toast Christmas and our trip. Our daughters, Kate and Jenny, said it was going to seem strange that for the first time in their memory we wouldn't be home for Christmas. I glanced at Jane, hoping that for her, we would indeed be home for Christmas after all.

Departure day. Jane's coat arrived from J. Crew in the nick of time, but it didn't fit. I persuaded her to take her mink coat for travel and evenings, the tent for exploring. Because we had so much luggage, I decided to leave the binoculars behind.

"We *need* the binoculars," Jane implored, and waved two guidebooks. "Hundreds of birds, especially seabirds on the coast. Wales is the wintering place for birds from all over Europe." I sighed and repacked the binocs.

We were at the door of our New York apartment, about to leave for the airport. "All set?" I asked.

"Wait!" Jane darted back into the bedroom, then returned with something wrapped in layers of tissue paper.

"What in God's name is *that*?" I snapped.

"A Christmas tree ornament."

"Just what we need. *Now* are you ready to go?"

Jane said she had been getting ready to go to Wales all her life.

CHAPTER THREE

Croeso i Gymru!

Michael Writes

After one night in London, we boarded the early-morning train at Paddington Station. We were traveling first class between London and Cardiff because I wanted to find out if it was anything close to the luxury train travel you see in English movies. Well, we didn't have one of those little compartments where people sit facing one another, but the seats were big and deep and there was a dining car, where one customer was already tucking into scrambled eggs and sausages and what looked suspiciously like an ale.

It is said that you can spot the difference between the English and the Welsh in these railroad cars. As you approach the Severn River—the boundary between the two countries—the English become more and more taciturn behind their newspapers; the Welsh, more gregarious. By the time the train passed into Wales, the carriages would hum with what the Welsh do best: talk.

The Welsh word for this gift of the gab is *hwyl*—part verbal exuberance, part poetry, part sheer hyperbole. Dylan Thomas had it. So did Richard Burton. Perhaps the most famous example is Owen Glendower in *Henry IV.* Glendower boasts to Hotspur: "I can call spirits from the vasty deep." Hotspur replies: "Why, so can I, or so can any man; but will they come . . . ?"

My wife is not only half Welsh; she has never gotten over being a high school cheerleader, and the combination can be overwhelming. I watched her expression as she listened to a couple near us chatting away in a language I couldn't recognize.

"Michael, just listen to that. It's the first time in my entire life that I've heard the Welsh language spoken in conversation."

I listened dutifully, if doubtfully. Jane leapt upon the couple and thanked them for the extraordinary experience they'd given her. "Welsh is such a beautiful language," she said. "So lilting. Even more musical than I thought."

The couple looked at her curiously and explained they had been speaking Greek.

Undeterred, Jane introduced herself to two young boys, Iestyn and Steven, who were studying Welsh in school and agreed to give her a lesson. It's remarkable that the Welsh language has survived as well as it has. Although less than 20 percent of the population speak it, Welsh is doing better than Scots or Irish Gaelic. And the most hopeful sign is the growing number of children studying and speaking it.

I listened to Jane's lesson: the colors. Black is *du,* pronounced "dee." Blue is *glas;* pronounced "glahz." Gold is *aur,* pronounced "eye-er." My wife the linguist looked startled. "*Aurum* is the Latin for gold. How come a Welsh word has a Latin root?" I suggested that we ask Nona. It became our theme for the rest of the stay: Nona will know. And Nona always did.

As we neared the Severn River, I thought that this would be an historic moment: Jane's first sight of the land of her forefathers. We dove into a tunnel dark as a mine shaft. When we came out, the first thing we saw was a sign in Welsh and English. *CROESO I GYMRU.* WELCOME TO WALES. (The Welsh word for Wales is *Cymru,* but the *C* changes to a *G* after the letter *I.* Nobody says Welsh is easy.)

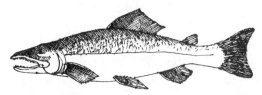

At Cardiff, we transferred from our big first-class train into a smaller one. There was no dining car, but a rosy young woman patrolled with a cart, selling tea, coffee, sandwiches, and wine. Jane and I shared a salmon-salad sandwich that had been nicely *pressed* in the English manner of tea sandwiches. It tasted wonderful. I ordered coffee. Jane, who takes on the protective coloration of whatever country she is in, had tea.

The landscape changed from gray to green; lambs were everywhere. At every station, the name of the town is inscribed in Welsh and English, so with the aid of a glossary, we began to pick out some Welsh words. We passed Penybont, Llanelli, Caerfyrddin. *Pen* is a headland; *llan,* a holy place; *caer,* a fort or stronghold. *Caer* is a familiar prefix in Wales, a country that built forts against its enemies as early as the Bronze Age. Anyone who has read Mary Stuart's Arthurian trilogy will recognize Caerleon, King Arthur's headquarters. Then there is Caerphilly, famous for its castle and its cheese. Cardiff, capital of Wales, is still *Caerdydd* in Welsh.

Nona met us at Haverfordwest at 2:30 in the afternoon. She looked more like an elf than a scholarly librarian—tiny, fey, full of lore. We all talked at once during the thirty-minute drive to St. David's. I knew then that the trip was going to be fun, even if Jane didn't find her family.

At St. David's, Nona gave us a quick tour before we checked in at the hotel. You don't see the cathedral at first; unlike many cathedrals, which are built on heights, this one is tucked away in a hollow. Most of the guidebooks say it was to hide the cathedral away from the marauding Vikings. I suspect otherwise. The Vikings weren't dumb; they raided this coast a dozen times or more in the Middle Ages and knew very well the cathedral was right there, with all its treasures. No, I bet the hollow was a holy place in pre-Christian times and the Christians simply built their temple on already-hallowed ground.

We passed the town stationery store, butcher shop, grocery, liquor store, bookshop. Suddenly, the cathedral popped up. It is a *masculine* cathedral, not lacy and feminine like the Gothic ones of France. Built of Cambrian sandstone from the cliffs not far south, the cathedral is an eerily beautiful light purple. Nona promised a complete tour on Saturday morning; she would not leave out a single stone.

Then, because the sun sets at four o'clock in late December, we needed to hurry in order to see the coast. We drove past the Warpool Court Hotel, originally built as the choir school for St. David's Cathedral in the 1860s. The hotel looked dark; Nona thought surely it was closed for the season.

"Too bad you won't get to see it. It's quite a lovely old place," Nona commented. "And there's another connection. Gail and David Lloyd—with one of David's brothers and his wife—ran the hotel for about fifteen years. It didn't return enough to support two growing families, and they had to sell it in 1985. A shame. Today the Warpool is one of the loveliest hotels in this part of Wales."

Jane turned to stare at the dark old building. "I spoke to the Lloyds just yesterday," Nona continued. "Gail said she is awfully curious about you." She paused. "And I suspect David is, too, even if he won't admit it."

"Oh, Nona, do you think there's even a chance that we're related?" Jane asked.

"Well, it's more than coincidence that you both have Lloyds *and* Thomases in your family tree,"

Nona said thoughtfully. "And when you're a Celt, you believe that anything is possible."

We drove past the site where St. Non gave birth to St. David, on a clifftop looking west toward the islands of Ramsey and Grassholm, themselves sacred in both Christian and pre-Christian legend. Nona's eyes shone and her small face was animated as though she was telling this story for the first time. The birth of St. David had been prophesied by Merlin and also by St. Patrick, who wanted to establish a monastery in Wales but was told by an angel that it was reserved for another. Luckily for Patrick, he was granted all of Ireland.

Nona told us that like so many places where there are Christian chapels sited near prehistoric remains, St. Non's has a holy well. Its waters are said to have sprung from the ground at the birth of David. The well is still visited by pilgrims and remains famous for its healing qualities. The sun began to sink into the bay. It was definitely teatime.

St. Non's Hotel is small, just two stories high, with a simply furnished dining room, an alcove for tea, and—its most appealing feature—a jolly pub. We ordered tea and Nona unpacked the bag of books she was lending us. She had books on the castles, churches, and monuments of Pembrokeshire; an anthology of Welsh poets and another of Welsh stories; a guide to the Pembrokeshire Coast National Park; a British Ordnance Guide to the famous coast walks; the program for Sunday's guided tour to the Preseli Hills; and the Christmas schedule for the cathedral.

Over tea, Jane asked Nona about the Welsh children's song Mim had taught her. "It was handed down from one generation of the family to the next, and it probably got garbled over the years. It may be just gibberish. It's *supposed* to mean 'Would you like to buy a broom, ma'am?'" Jane sang a few lines.

> *Gwella king ah, key burnee skeebit,*
> *Burnee skeebit, burnee skeebit.*

Nona listened hard. "Once more?" Jane sang the lines again. "I don't think it's gibberish at all," Nona said. "In Welsh, *ysgubell* is pronounced '*skeebeth*.' It means 'broom.'"

"*Skeebeth*," Jane repeated softly. She looked as though someone had given her an early Christmas present.

Just before Nona left, she sprang her biggest surprise. Would we like to join the carolers on Christmas Eve? Jane said we would love to but that we didn't feel up to the four-part harmony. "Oh," Nona explained, "we aren't inviting you to *sing*. You haven't had the chance to rehearse. But we thought you'd like to go along with us and pass the hat."

It was just a little after five o'clock now, but pitch-dark as Jane and I explored the town on foot. It was quiet except for a pub, where even at this early hour we could hear merriment. A signboard on a stone fence with an arrow announced:

200 YARDS TO THE
WARPOOL COURT HOTEL. OPEN. POOL.
TENNIS COURT. SEASIDE VIEWS.

"Let's see if it really is open," Jane said. "We could have a sherry there before dinner."

The country lane heading to the Warpool Court Hotel had no lights, so we shuffled along cautiously, hoping no cars would come by. None did. There were no sounds except for a brook beside the road and some animal noises that could have been cows. We went through a gate and saw the hotel, which looked dark and empty. Two steps more and the courtyard was flooded with light as we tripped an automatic switch. We opened the door and went into the foyer.

A young woman appeared, introduced herself as Zoë, and told us the hotel was indeed open. There were no guests yet, but quite a few were expected to arrive tomorrow for the three-day holiday. She showed us into the bar, poured two sherries, and lighted the fire in the big fireplace. Jane sighed. I've been married to her long enough to know exactly what she was thinking. Could we possibly stay *here*?

"Actually, we have a few rooms that haven't been booked yet," Zoë offered, perfectly on cue. "There is a package price for the three nights, including bed, breakfast, and dinner, but since it's the last minute, I could give you a special rate of twenty-five pounds per person, just bed and breakfast."

The front door banged and a blast of cold air made the fire leap. A man came in with strands of dark green ivy. He climbed a bar stool and arranged them over the mantel.

"It's not symmetrical," I objected. He looked surprised.

"My husband is an architect," Jane explained. "He can't help himself."

We introduced ourselves. The ivy-bearer was Peter Trier, one of the hotel's owners. He and I remounted bar stools and fussed with the ivy until it was perfect. Zoë mentioned that we were thinking about staying here at the Warpool Court. Peter made our decision for us. "Then you have to stay in The Nursery."

He led us upstairs to inspect a delightful room on the third floor. "Gloriously sunny by day," Peter explained, "with views out over the formal gardens to St. Bride's Bay and the offshore islands." The real charm of The Nursery was its hundreds of hand-painted tiles, all pinks and blues and greens, recounting children's tales and flower allegories.

"I'd like to wake up here every morning," I told Jane, who knew I was going to say that.

Downstairs in the bar again, Peter invited us to have another sherry and told us the story of Ada Williams and her tiles. The choir school, by then a country manor, was Ada's home in the late 1800s.

She spent thirty years painting these tiles. Most of them, like the ones on either side of the fireplace in the bar, trace the genealogy of her family, using heraldry and Celtic illumination. Her best work, in Peter's opinion, was done on the tiles in The Nursery.

We told Peter and Zoë we were too tired to move our luggage that night but would check in tomorrow. Then we retraced our steps down the dark country road, back to town and St. Non's Hotel.

It had been a long time since we shared that salmon-salad sandwich on the train. In the hotel's pub, I ordered a steak; Jane, a baked sea bass. The steak was good and rare; the fish was moist, the way she likes it. With the entrées came big bowls of cauliflower, beans, fried potatoes, and salad. After dinner, we sipped our wine and Jane challenged me to a game of darts.

She picked up three of those heavy pub-style darts that look so lethal. "Don't throw them. *Push* them," I instructed. To my surprise, she placed all three in the center circle, then declared she would quit while she was ahead. It was only nine o'clock, but it had been a long day, full of discoveries.

Jane fell asleep immediately and the next morning told me she had dreamed about brooms. I woke once, a few minutes before two, heard a bell strike the hour, and realized it was the one in the cathedral tower. I went back to sleep, and I don't think I dreamed about anything at all.

CHAPTER FOUR

Christmas Eve

Michael Writes

Breakfast was served in the pub. Did we want a "cooked breakfast"? We did, and proceeded to eat eggs, sausage, toast with marmalade, and coffee.

I had a talk with Sandy Falconer, owner of St. Non's Hotel, and explained that the architecture and nursery tiles of the Warpool Court had seduced me. Sandy was understanding, but he pointed out that he would have to charge us for the three-day package anyway, since it was too late for him to rebook our room. I knew this wouldn't sit well with Jane, who thought we were getting off scot-free, but Sandy and I struck a bargain. He would reduce the package a tad and we would take our dinners at St. Non's for the duration of the package.

We asked Becky, the attractive young woman at the desk, to call us a taxi for Fishguard. She said it would arrive in ten minutes. "This is the first day in two weeks we've had sunshine instead of rain. Did you bring it from America?" It was sunny but very cold as we climbed into the taxi, Jane in her duck hunter's jacket, I in my J. Crew coat, and both of us in our matching moccasins. We were ready for a brisk walk around Dinas Island, part of the Pembrokeshire Coast National Park.

The Coast path snakes along the sea for about two hundred miles—most of it close to the edge of the cliffs. The guidebooks agree that although the path is generally suitable for casual walkers of all ages, it does have dangerous patches now and then. And every guide cautions walkers not to be caught on the paths after sundown!

For Jane and me, the seabird population was a big attraction of this part of Wales. We had read of the "teeming colonies" that nest on the cliffs. We were sure to see razorbills—the official bird of the park—cormorants, oystercatchers, fulmars, puffins, guillemots, gannets, and Manx shearwaters. One writer promised that it is "in winter that the coast of Wales holds the greatest number and variety of birds" and was home to *huge numbers* of waders—ducks, Greenland geese, and whooper swans. As bird people, we were ready to be enchanted. So at Jane's urging, I went back to our room at the last minute and slung the binoculars around my neck.

The taxi driver commented on the fine weather. "Bring it with you, did you?"

We picked up our car near Fishguard at a garage that doubles as service station and rental-car agency. As Nona had instructed, we drove down to the old part of town, which had been the setting for the movie *Under Milk Wood*. We walked along the quays and, playing an old favorite game of ours, I asked Jane which boat she would like to own. "There's a cute little blue one over there, just about your size." Jane wasn't buying my banter.

"I'm cold," she said, stamping her feet and blowing on her hands. "My feet are numb. My hands are numb."

Uh-oh, I thought. The last time Jane was this cold was in Normandy not too long ago. We had rented a cottage on the corniche above the English Channel. It was a picturesque place, ivy-covered, bucolic, heatless. Jane woke me up at midnight our first night there. "I'm cold," she said. "My feet are numb."

"Do you want more blankets?" I asked sympathetically.

"I want to go home," she replied. We left for New York the next morning. So I always worry a little when Jane is cold.

We drove into the main shopping area of Fishguard, which was busy with last-minute Christmas shoppers, and found a shoe store. Jane explained her problem to a sympathetic young woman, who suggested a pair of "shoe liners." The package copy promised they would keep feet "toasty warm," so we bought them and a pair of immensely thick socks.

Jane walked stiff-legged out of the shoe store. "I feel like a knight in full armor," she said. "If I fell down, I wouldn't be able to get up again without a crane." Just a few stores down the street, we found a pair of bright red mittens made of Welsh wool, which Jane put on *under* her leather gloves. "Two cranes and a hoist," she amended.

We decided to have a light lunch before tackling Dinas Island; we chose The Royal Oak, whose sign proclaimed it was the HOME OF THE FISHGUARD PIE. We asked Pauline Matthews, chef and wife of the publican, what goes into a Fishguard pie.

Pauline looked shocked at our question. "Well, dears, if I gave you the whole recipe, it wouldn't be our secret anymore, would it?" She did confide that you combine shrimp, flaked codfish, leeks, and mushrooms in a wine-spiked cream sauce and then bake it under puff pastry. "But, mind, I'm holding back one important ingredient."

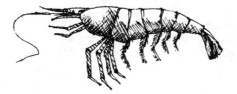

Jane and I shared an order of Fishguard pie. The cod was fresh and zesty, caught that morning at Solva. I'm a pretty good cook, so I was only a bite or two into the pie before I knew that the missing ingredient in Pauline's recipe was dill.

After lunch, it was time for Dinas Island. "This wonderful little walk," as one guidebook described it, is deemed suitable for the entire family, as long as a bit of care is taken with small children where the

path skirts sheer drops to the sea. We read, too, that
Needle Rock, a sea stack just off the island, is a
thriving bird colony.

We scrambled up the path, if it could be called a
path at all. Actually, it was only a narrow rut scored
by the recent weeks of heavy rain. You had to place
one foot directly in front of another, tightrope-
style. Every time you lifted one foot, an overshoe of
mud would adhere. Writing of this same path,
Welsh poet Peter Finch talked of leaving boot
marks "like fossils in the fluid mud." He added, "I
get the feeling that if there is an edge to this world
then it is here."

It was slow, slippery going. I swore at the binoc-

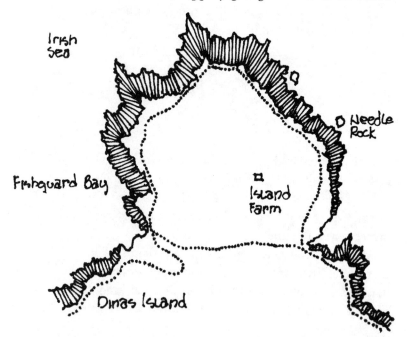

ulars, which swung and bumped against my chest.
Jane squished and sloshed and muttered behind me.
Suddenly, the path was only inches from the very
edge of the cliff. The drop to the sea was straight
down to a bunch of evil-looking rocks. "My God,"
Jane said. "What a wonderful little walk, so suitable
for the whole family!"

After an hour of walking, we were only halfway
around the island. It was after three o'clock, less
than an hour to go before dark. We could turn back
and retrace our steps or keep going. I suggested that
we go on, since the path might get better. Jane
agreed. "And anyway," she added, "as long as we've
come this far, I want to see all those birds on Needle
Rock."

The brook that had been running beside the path
now changed its course. Brook and path became
one. We kept walking, ankle-deep in icy water. The
moccasins were sodden; it was like walking bare-
foot. In another fifteen minutes, we finally arrived
at Needle Rock. There were no birds.

We had come almost full circle. "My feet are
cold," Jane said. "*And* they hurt, too."

"We're almost back to the car," I told her. "We
can take this shortcut across the field. Five minutes."

Five minutes later, we were surrounded by Welsh
sheep and tall fences in the middle of somebody's
farm. Smoke came from the farmhouse chimney; it
was the first sign of civilization we had seen in
hours. "We can just climb over the fence and pick
up the path to the car," I suggested cheerfully.

Jane said she was not going to climb any fence. We were lost and she was going to ask for help! She marched to the farmhouse and rang the bell. A little boy opened the door. "Hello," Jane greeted him. "We're from New York and we're lost."

His parents told us we could take their private roadway, which would lead us back to our car. "Don't mind the sheep," they advised. "They're just curious."

Escorted by five sheep, we walked to the car. Just as I put the binoculars into their case, a lone bird flew by. We thought it was a puffin. "Are you game for a few more coast walks?" I asked.

"Oh, as long as they are all sweet little jaunts like this one." Jane chuckled. "As long as I can find two large Band-Aids for the blisters forming on both my heels. I *adore* walking in icy water, darling. I'll be at your side."

Back in St. David's, it was early evening as we moved our luggage from St. Non's Hotel to the Warpool Court, just in time to meet Nona for the Christmas Eve caroling.

Jane Writes

The carolers assembled at the home of Larry Richardson, a retired St. David's policeman. Larry welcomed us, offered hot punch, and introduced us to the group as "the Americans who are going to pass the hat." There were twelve or fifteen carolers, including Larry's son and daughter. Stephen is an opera singer and Mandy, a tall, pretty seventeen-year-old blonde, is still in high school. "Dad has kept the cathedral choir well stocked," Stephen told me. "At one point, there were six Richardsons singing in it." Nona introduced us to Andrew Lamb, organist scholar at the cathedral and a tenor. "I'm Welsh through and through," he said proudly.

The singers warmed up with a few carols. The Richardson children were outstanding. Mandy had a high, clear soprano voice; Stephen, a magnificent bass. Everyone paused a few moments to watch the television set—King's College Choir telecast from Cambridge. Larry explained that the first note of the opening hymn is traditionally sung by a young choirboy. Until the choirmaster turns and points at him, no boy knows who will be chosen to sing that first high, sweet Christmas note.

The city was quiet, the streets empty and the houses seemingly dark. But as soon as the carols began, doors opened and people stood just inside or came out to listen. The carolers sang all the old favorites: "It Came Upon the Midnight Clear," "Good King Wenceslas," "O Come, All Ye Faithful," and "Silent Night"—all the carols of my Lewisburg childhood. Mandy's voice floated over the city. "Listen, Mim," I whispered. "Welsh singing in a Welsh valley."

Michael and I rang bells, knocked on doors, and passed the hat. It was actually a hat—in fact, Larry

Richardson's hat, which he took off his own head and handed to me when we realized nobody had brought a container for the collection.

"Something for the cathedral choir?" I would ask. And because St. David's is really a small town, most people saw that Michael and I were strangers, wondered why we were with the carolers, and found out the story. Before the caroling was over, half the population knew we were the Americans from New York who had come to find their family.

We left the carolers and went to have something to eat at St. Non's Hotel before going to midnight Mass at the cathedral. Dinner hour was long over, but the staff knew we were caroling and had promised to keep a meal warm for us. We had minestrone soup, hot and welcome, roast beef for Michael, and Welsh lamb for me. Sandy Falconer appeared, poured red wine, and joined us for a glass.

The hotel guests were gathered around the piano in the lounge, singing carols at first, then old favorites. The piano broke into "New York, New York" suddenly, and the Welsh stopped singing. Nobody knew the words. I couldn't resist. After all, I had headed the "I Love New York" advertising campaign. If I couldn't sing "New York, New York," who could? I belted it out.

"Let's have an American medley," a man called, and we all sang "California, Here I Come," "Chicago," and "I Left My Heart in San Francisco." The man who had requested the medley knew all the words. I complimented him.

"I love the States," he said. "Go there every chance I get." We introduced ourselves. He was David Barnett, a doctor from England, here for the holiday with his family. He had been coming to St. David's for Christmas every year since he was a boy. We said we would very likely bump into one another at the hotel's gala dinner and dance on Boxing Day.

"Michael has his black tie all ready," I said in parting. David looked blank. Was it possible they called it something else?

The cathedral was packed for the 11:30 P.M. service: the first Communion of Christmas. A man seated next to me shook my hand and wished me a merry Christmas. "Harry," he said, introducing himself. "Jane," I replied.

"You and your husband were at my door with the carolers. Welcome to Wales. Hope you will find your family." I was stunned.

Nona came in with her family and blew a kiss. Andrew Lamb, headed for his organ, spotted us and grinned. While Andrew played the introit, the choir assembled. They wore red robes with stiff white-ruffed collars and carried lighted candles. Many of them, our caroling friends, waved and smiled.

They launched into "O Come, All Ye Faithful" and headed down the aisle. Mandy's voice again soared over the others, and over the organ. You would never guess she had been singing out in the cold streets for the past three hours.

The dean read from the Gospel According to St. Luke.

And, lo, the angel of the Lord came upon them, and the glory of the Lord shone round about them: and they were sore afraid. And the angel said unto them, Fear not: for, behold, I bring you good tidings of great joy, which shall be to all people.

The dean spoke briefly and simply. During the Peace, when the congregation exchanged greetings, people we didn't know smiled and nodded at us and wished us *Nadolig Llawen*—Merry Christmas. We received Communion and sang "Hark! the Herald Angels Sing."

Then we walked through the town, darker and quieter than ever, back under the alley of trees to the Warpool Court and up to The Nursery.

"Merry Christmas, Michael," I said. "Thank you for bringing me to Wales."

"*Nadolig Llawen,*" he replied. "And you're welcome."

CHAPTER FIVE

Christmas Day

Jane Writes

There may be no better way to invoke the Christmas mornings of childhood than to wake up in a nursery. It was still dark and Michael was sound asleep, so I put on my bathrobe, plugged in the electric kettle, made a cup of tea, and, cup in hand, explored the painted tiles that covered the walls.

The wall facing the bed is devoted to "The Tourney of the Lily and the Rose," illustrating the old nursery tale with Victorian flourishes. The other three walls are even more fun: a giant flower allegory all green and pink and yellow, interwoven with cupids and heraldry, swags and garlands. Ada Williams certainly had more fun painting the tiles in the nursery than she did the genealogical ones in the lounge downstairs.

Michael woke up and we gravely wished each other a merry Christmas. No exchange of presents; we had agreed the trip to Wales was our

gift to each other this year. Downstairs for breakfast, we stood at the tall windows in the sunny dining room and had our first daylight look at the
hotel's formal Italian gardens and the view past St.
Non's well to St. Bride's Bay. If you went straight
west from here, you'd land in Ireland.

Two women guests were standing near us at the
windows and we introduced ourselves. They were
Miss Myra Evans and Miss Mary Smart, retired
schoolteachers from Cardiff. Miss Myra was all
Welsh, she told us; Miss Mary only half. I offered
up the fact that my family were Thomases and
Lloyds. "Oh, we'll let *you* in." Miss Myra beamed.

Miss Myra was tall and plump and placid,
dressed in a soft lilac silk that reminded me of my
grandmother's dresses. Miss Mary was short and
energetic, ramrod straight, military in her bearing.
Even her crisp white hair did her bidding. The
women had been friends for almost fifty years and
their roles were established: Miss Mary was the
feisty sheepdog to Miss Myra's amiable, intelligent
Welsh sheep.

We made small talk about the weather; this was
the second brilliant day in a row. "It is extraordinary to have days of sunshine like this," Miss Myra
commented. "Mary and I have been coming to St.
David's on Christmas holidays for ten years now."

"Eleven," Miss Mary corrected.

Waitresses began to bustle about and we found a
table set for two, with our names on place cards.
The breakfast menu was formidable: In addition
to the expected ham and eggs and sausages, there

were kippers, tomatoes, mushrooms, and halibut. Michael ordered kippers, reminding me that he had not eaten kippers in thirty-five years. The first year of our marriage, I cooked kippers for one Sunday breakfast and told Michael that they smelled so awful, I would never, never make them again. And I never did.

I looked over at the teachers, sitting at *their* little table for two and had an idea. "Michael, would it be okay with you if I invited them to join us for Christmas dinner?"

Michael said it was a terrific idea. "You are being so dear to me." I thanked him. Intensely private person that he is, back home he would have vetoed the idea. But he wanted my Christmas Day to be as perfect as he could help make it.

Miss Mary and Miss Myra said they would love to join us. They were going to the eleven o'clock service at the cathedral and we agreed to meet in the bar lounge for a sherry when they returned.

"Twelve-fifteen," Miss Myra said, smiling.

"Twelve-thirty," said Miss Mary.

Done.

Michael and I set off for the cathedral and the 9:30 service in Welsh: *Cymun y Nadolig.* Welsh is a melodious language that can be a harp one minute, an organ the next. I followed the service as well as I could in the Welsh-English prayer book. *Almighty God,* for example, rolls out as *Hollalluog Dduw.* God must have to pay attention when a Welshman speaks to Him.

The hymnal was in Welsh only, so I didn't know

what we would sing until the music began. "*O deuwch ac addolwn*" turned out to be "O Come, All Ye Faithful." One word in the fourth stanza really baffled me: *Ymgnawdoledig.* Nona translated it for me later; it means "incarnate."

The vicar, a tall man with huge hands, celebrated this service for our little congregation of seventeen people. I couldn't follow his sermon, of course, but caught the word *Nadolig* several times as he gestured to the congregation. I think he was urging us at Christmas to be as good as we could be—another chop of those big compelling hands, or else.

After the service, the vicar came over and shook hands, turned to greet other parishioners, and then, as we began to walk away, rushed back to put an arm around each of us. "You're the Americans from New York! I'm sorry this is such a busy day for me. Any other day of the year and I'd invite you for tea," he said. "Or something stronger."

Back at the Warpool Court, we were suddenly aware that other guests and members of the staff were behaving oddly. Do you remember the scene in *Casablanca* when Humphrey Bogart helps the young Yugoslavian couple to win at roulette so they have enough money to go to the United States? Then his staff all beam at him mistily. That's the treatment we were getting.

"You're having dinner with Miss Evans and Miss Smart," Peter Trier said approvingly. "So nice. So Christmasy. I wish more people would do that."

In the bar lounge, Zoë poured us sherry. "Miss

Evans and Miss Smart aren't back from the cathedral service yet, but they'll be here soon. They are *so* pleased." The bartender smiled at us. So did guests at two of the other tables. My spur-of-the-moment invitation was clearly a hit in St. David's.

Later, as the four of us walked into the dining room, I could feel silent applause. We were given a big round table, the place of honor, right in front of the windows. Michael ordered a bottle of champagne and we looked at the Christmas menu. One could begin with tomato and basil soup, salmon, smoked on the premises, or oysters. There was traditional roast Pembrokeshire turkey, ordered by all three of us ladies, and roast goose, Michael's choice.

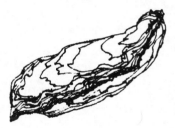

While we waited for our first course, the conversation turned to Welsh food. Miss Myra told us that the most typical Welsh foods are those of the poor. For one dish called *sgotyn,* the recipe goes like this. Take a piece of bread, slice it into a bowl, pour boiling water over it, add seasonings, and eat.

Miss Mary sniffed. "*Sgotyn* is from the *north* of Wales."

Michael poured the champagne.

Miss Myra dabbed her moist cheek with a lady-like lace handkerchief and continued, undeterred. "And then there are the famous Welsh cakes." She gave us her recipe. "In the good old days, you cooked them on a hearthstone and then you spread them with butter."

"I use a frying pan," Miss Myra said. "And spread them with *jam.*"

We went on to discuss *cawl* (pronounced "*cow-ell*"), a thick, hearty soup traditionally made with neck of lamb and root vegetables. Now it was Miss Mary's turn to describe the recipe. "Just before serving, you top it with grated cheese and put it under the grill."

"I top my cawl with *dumplings* and cheese," Miss Myra added softly.

Miss Mary shook her head. "Cheese only."

We ate our tomato and basil soup and began on our roast turkey. Michael poured more champagne.

"I don't usually have strong drink in the middle of the day," Miss Mary said.

"But this is only once a year," Miss Myra said, lifting her glass to us, "and anyway, champagne isn't strong drink."

Point for Miss Myra.

They told us about their teaching careers, spent mostly in one-room schoolhouses in mining valleys. I asked whether the men and boys would really sing at the end of the day as they came home from the mine.

"Oh, indeed they would sing," Miss Myra said. "Not every day. But if one fellow started, they'd all join in. Fine singing, it was."

"The best singing," said Miss Mary, "was at funerals."

Michael ordered a bottle of wine.

"It's like something out of *How Green Was My Valley*," I said. "Do you know there's a special note in your voices when you talk about those days?"

"Well, we have a special word for it in Wales," Miss Myra told me. "*Hiraeth*. It means a nostalgia for Welsh days gone by, a lament for lost things."

"*Hiraeth*," I repeated. "It even sounds sad."

We looked at the menus again, this time for the dessert selections. The lemon syllabub was described as "a refreshing combination of lemon confit, Cointreau, and cream."

Mary Smart was delighted. "I wasn't going to order dessert after this enormous meal. But a lemon syllabub! Well, I'll have to try that."

Our waiter informed us that, alas, the syllabub had proved such a popular selection that there was no more to be had. Miss Mary looked crestfallen.

"Oh dear," I said, taking up my role as hostess. "It's because we were all so busy talking. We should have ordered dessert sooner. I feel awful about it."

"Don't feel awful for a single minute," Miss Myra ordered.

"Not for a single *second*," Miss Mary added. They nodded agreeably at each other and decided on the Christmas pudding. I had a taste of Miss

Myra's. It was exactly like the one Aunt Lib used to douse with brandy all year long.

The young chef of the Warpool Court, Mark Strangward, hurried into the dining room to inquire about our desserts. News had traveled fast. He told the ladies he would personally prepare a lemon syllabub for them that evening.

"Well, after all that food, I, for one, am going for a nice brisk walk!" Miss Mary announced in the "Quick, march" tones of a teacher who expects obedience.

The Christmas pudding had strengthened Miss Myra's resolve. "And *I* am going up for a nap."

A nap seemed like a good idea to us, as well. But before doing that, I called St. Non's Hotel and asked for our acquaintance of the evening before, Dr. David Barnett. The schoolteachers had made Christmas Day such a family affair, I hoped the Barnett family wouldn't mind if we shared their table on Boxing Day night. David was enthusiastic.

"Are you planning to wear black tie? A tuxedo?" I asked. "I gather that's the tradition here for Boxing Day."

"If it is, I've never heard of it," David said. "I'll be wearing the most formal clothes I brought with me—a sweater and trousers—what you Americans call 'slacks.'"

I told Michael he could repack his black tie and his dancing shoes. We wouldn't need them after all.

On an impulse, I called the Lloyd family. David answered, sounding gruff. I identified myself and said we were simply calling to wish them a happy holiday and were looking forward to seeing them on Monday. "Is this a bad moment to call you?"

"Well, not the best moment, I would say. You know how it is on Christmas Day. We are concentrating on our family."

There was a pause. I think he knew he had hurt my feelings without being quite sure why. "Well, Happy Christmas," David said. And just before he hung up, he added, "We are looking forward to seeing you, too."

We didn't take naps after all, reading instead about the Preseli Hills and St. Govan's Chapel and exchanging bits of information about sights we must see. Around seven, Michael went down to the buffet and came back up with turkey sandwiches. Miss Myra and Miss Mary, he reported, were having a lemon syllabub.

It had been a wonderful Christmas Day, but I vaguely felt that something was lacking, something I hadn't missed in a long, long time. Then, just as I was falling asleep, I heard Aunt Lib's voice and knew what it was: poetry.

MISS MYRA'S WELSH CAKES

8 ounces self-rising flour
4 ounces butter
4 ounces sugar
pinch of cinnamon
one large egg, beaten
4 ounces sultanas or currants

Mix flour, butter, and sugar together until you have fine crumbs. Add cinnamon. Make a well in the center and pour in the beaten egg and sultanas or currants. Mix into a firm dough, then roll out to form about a one-half-inch-thick sheet and cut into little rounds. Cook on a heated griddle until they are a nice golden brown—not too dark. Spread with butter.

Makes 12 cakes

MISS MARY'S *CAWL*, OR WELSH SOUP

2 onions
4 carrots
1 yellow turnip
1/2 bunch of celery
4 potatoes
1 leek (save the green
  for garnish)

1 tablespoon flour
2 ounces butter
2 pounds neck of lamb
salt and pepper
meat or vegetable stock
  to cover

Peel and dice the vegetables, coat them with flour, and brown lightly in melted butter. Add the lamb, season, cover with stock, and gently simmer for three hours or until cooked. Skim off fat from time to time. Remove meat and cut it into dice. Before serving, add the green diced leeks and bring to a boil. Pour into ovenproof serving bowl, top with grated cheese, and brown under the broiler.

Serves 4 to 6

WARPOOL COURT LEMON SYLLABUB

2 lemons	*6 ounces sugar*
3 ounces butter	*1/2 ounce cornstarch*
4 eggs	*1 1/2 pints heavy cream*

Combine lemon juice, grated lemon rind, and all other ingredients except the cream. Cook over low heat in a stainless-steel saucepan until the sauce is thick enough to coat a wooden spoon. Allow to cool. Whip the cream until it holds peaks. Combine cream and sauce and pour into wineglasses. Chill until served.

Serves 4

CHAPTER SIX

Boxing Day

Michael Writes

 I was looking forward to this morning. Nona had volunteered to give us a special tour of the cathedral, her particular domain. It was like having Queen Elizabeth offer to show you around Buckingham Palace.

Before we met her, we stopped at the pharmacy in the center of town to buy Band-Aids for the blisters on both of Jane's heels. She was still wearing the new moccasins, even though they hurt her, because they were the only walking shoes she'd brought with her. "Damn it," she muttered. "Why didn't I bring my jogging shoes?"

"Right after the cathedral tour, we'll go to a shoe store and buy you the most comfortable, most waterproof walking boots in all of Wales," I consoled her.

The pharmacy was the only shop in town that was open, and we asked why. The woman behind the counter raised her eyebrows in surprise. "Today is Boxing Day! Almost as important a holiday as Christmas. By law, the only shops allowed to be open are those essential for people's health or well-being. Like a pharmacy."

"Not a shoe store?" Jane asked forlornly.

The woman shook her head. "Not a shoe store in all of Wales."

In the car, Jane applied the Band-Aids and put her socks and shoes back on. We drove to the cathedral and I watched as she walked gingerly, stiff-legged so her shoes wouldn't rub up and down, to the cathedral door, where Nona was waiting.

We stood in the sunshine, squinting up at the great west front of the building. Nona began. "St. David founded his monastery on this spot in the sixth century. I believe he felt an *energy source* here that was pre-Christian—possibly Bronze Age." Nona's voice was hushed. "The two main altars of the cathedral are both built over blind springs. If you hold a pendulum over one, it will begin to *swing*! You can feel the power. I know; I've done it."

Jane and Nona exchanged glances. This was the kind of mystic, Celtic, otherworldly stuff they both thrive on. If a table had been handy right then, they would have sat down and started it tipping.

Nona pointed out the impressive ruins of the Bishop's Palace. "A bishop of the cathedral won a 'privilege' from the Pope in 1123. Two pilgrimages to St. David's were the equivalent of one pilgrimage

to Rome. Well, pilgrims began to come in droves, and many of them were quite important chaps. So the Bishop's Palace was built as a place to entertain them."

Nona's two-hour tour covered every nook and cranny of the cathedral, and her running commentary was a blend of information, mysticism, and humor. We ended in the choir stalls, with their amazing wood carvings. Nona pointed to one, the head of a man, his mouth open in an anguished howl. "Most people think he's a sinner on his way to hell. But he's really a green man, a pagan spirit of the wood. And he's not in pain; he probably just drank too much wine."

Back outside, Jane and I gave Nona a round of applause. She smiled her thanks, then became serious. "I think we should leave quite early tomorrow morning for the Preseli Hills walk. I'm not absolutely sure of the route, and we don't want to risk arriving late and missing our group and the guide."

"I'm afraid my feet aren't up to it," Jane said glumly. "Just ambling around the cathedral has made me realize how much these shoes hurt. I'm so sorry."

Nona's face fell. "Oh, you can't miss the Preseli walk!" she protested fiercely. "Here's an idea. I have an old pair of true walking boots at home that will probably fit you."

Jane looked at Nona's tiny feet. "I think your feet are a good two sizes smaller than mine."

"Oh, those aren't *my* boots," Nona rejoined. "I have my own. No, I bought those at a yard sale just two weeks ago."

"What made you buy another pair of boots that wouldn't even fit you?" Jane asked.

"I just stood there and looked at them and knew that somebody was going to need them very badly, very soon," Nona told her. They exchanged one of their "table-tipping" glances.

Nona's charming little home, the Treasurer's House, is right in the cathedral close. She introduced us to her eleven-year-old son, Siôn, who was watching television and eating Christmas cookies, like any American kid on a school vacation. Nona bustled about, brought us mugs of tea, and fetched the boots. Jane put them on. They were hard, well-worn leather boots with thick heels, high, roomy toes, and yard-long laces that went through an intricate system of eyelets and clasps, then twice around Jane's ankles before ending up with a double bow in the front.

"How do they feel?" Nona asked.

"I could dance all night." Jane demonstrated. "They feel marvelous. I'm ready for another cliff walk!"

That's exactly what we did. We had a crab sandwich at the Warpool Court and set out along the coast path for Solva, three miles away as the crow

flies, more than twice that distance on the twisting
path. Most of Wales was out for an afternoon walk.
We passed whole families, from toddlers who had
to be helped over stiles to elderly gentlemen in plus
fours and cardigans, stomping along with walking
sticks. Holiday spirit was in the air. People smiled
and wished us "Happy Christmas!" and we returned the greeting.

The spell of bright sunny weather, now in its
fourth day, made the Welsh giddy with pleasure.
The December afternoon was almost warm enough
to make the ocean look inviting. Jane peered down
at the waves. "I'd like to dunk my feet just to see
how cold it is."

"There's no way to get down to it," I warned.
"And anyway, by the time you unlaced your boots
and laced them back up again, it would be dark."

Two hours later, just before sunset, we arrived in
Solva. It's a little fishing village that supplies much
of the fish and shellfish to local fish markets and
restaurants. Mark Strangward told us later that the
crabmeat we ate for lunch had come from Solva that
morning.

One shop in town was open and doing a brisk business in handmade lace and souvenirs. "That doesn't look very essential to health or well-being," Jane protested.

"I bet if we looked hard, we could find a shoe store open somewhere," I suggested.

"Oh, no," she said. "I won't give up my boots!"

We went into the little hotel overlooking the marina and the roar of voices led us straight to its pub, noisy, crowded, and full of laughter. At the bar, I ordered Welsh ale for myself, white wine for Jane, then looked around for a place to sit. A man in his fifties, wearing a tweed jacket I coveted, motioned to us that there were seats at his table. We joined his little group and introduced ourselves. Frank Lamb was the tweedy one; the other four were Chris, Muriel, and Albert Anstrey and their older sister, Shirley Anstrey Pierce. There were the expressions of surprise and interest we'd come to expect whenever people learned we were Americans and why we had come to Wales. Jane asked whether they all lived in Solva.

"I'm the only one who lives here now," Shirley Pierce explained. "They're visiting me for the holidays. I invited them months ago to come and stay with me in my new home, but it didn't get finished in time, so they have to stay here at the inn."

Everyone laughed, as though that was the best joke in the world. Shirley told us without a touch of self-pity that she was a recent widow. She and her husband had always talked about all the places in the world where they might retire. "But when he died, the only place I thought about was coming back home to Solva."

"Of course you're back here, old girl," Frank Lamb said quietly. "This is where you first learned to stand on your own two feet. And this is where you'll learn to stand on them again."

We finished our drinks, wished the Anstreys and Frank Lamb a happy Christmas, and walked over to the bar. I asked the bartender how we could find a taxi to take us back to St. David's; he volunteered to call one for us. He was back in a moment. "All booked up." He shrugged. "Holiday season. Sorry."

"Well, would you call a *different* taxi, please," Jane persisted. "We're getting sort of late."

"There's only the one taxi in Solva," the bartender told her sorrowfully.

Jane was unruffled. "How long will we have to wait for it?"

"Three to four hours."

My wife persisted. "Maybe there's a student around here who would like to earn a few pounds for driving us back?"

"I'll drive you to St. David's." It was Frank Lamb. "I haven't had a drink yet and I've an hour to spare. I'm your man."

When we pulled into the courtyard of the hotel, we thanked Frank for his kindness to strangers.

"No thanks needed," he said. "Next time you see some folks who look like they need a lift, give it to them."

"I will," I promised. And I have.

Michael and I dressed for the Boxing Day dinner and dance at St. Non's Hotel. We decided to be conservative, so we chose the same outfits we had worn on Christmas Day—a blue suit for Michael, a blue knit suit for me.

The dining room of the Warpool Court was filled with flowers and candlelight, and our fellow caroler, the cathedral's organist, Andrew Lamb, was at the piano. Miss Myra and Miss Mary, about to sit down for dinner, expressed their delight.

"Andrew Lamb is so talented." Miss Myra smiled. "I do so hope people will be quiet while he plays during dinner."

"Of course they will be quiet." Miss Mary frowned. "I shall insist upon it."

We left the Warpool Court to Andrew Lamb playing Mozart and entered St. Non's to the sounds of a trio playing "Don't Cry for Me, Argentina." What a strange song to be playing here in St. David's on Boxing Day. I thought perhaps it was somebody's special request, but next the trio swung into "If I Were A Bell" from *Guys and Dolls.* Clearly, they were playing a medley of show tunes, mixing eras at random.

The crowd seemed to be the same people who had gathered around the piano to sing on Christmas Eve, but tonight they were more sedate, taking their places quietly at the tables. The group was more English than Welsh, and younger than the clientele of the Warpool Court. One lone couple, white-haired and in their seventies, was on the dance floor. He was the only man in the room in a dinner jacket, she the only woman in a long gown. They danced serenely, not speaking, a reminder of an era when it was considered boorish not to dance with your partner before dinner.

"Good evening, Mrs. Maas, Mr. Maas." It was pretty Becky, the young woman who had been at the reception desk when we arrived. I complimented her for remembering our name.

"Oh, your name is a watchword in our house these days. I'm Becky *Lloyd,* and it's my parents you're going to stay with on Monday and Tuesday. Mummy is testing recipes for your grand dinner and Dad does nothing but plan what poetry they'll all read."

"Poetry?" I repeated in surprise, feeling that David Lloyd had, in some uncanny way, read my thoughts.

"He's having a little eisteddfod—a poetry reading and perhaps some singing—in your honor. He believes you like poetry."

"I love poetry," I said. "But how does your father know that?"

"He said you must like it, because you are Welsh."

After Becky left, Michael smiled at me. "I think your Mr. David Lloyd is more pleased about your coming than he's letting on."

The Barnett family arrived and we found our

table. The Barnett's son, about twelve years old, told me he had been here on Christmas Eve when I led the crowd in singing "New York, New York." "You're an actress, aren't you," he said. It was a statement, not a question. I told him I was.

"What have you been in?"

I thought back to the last play I did, at Bucknell University in 1953. "*Oedipus Rex.*"

"I haven't seen it," he said unhappily. "Is it new? Would I know the music?"

"Actually, it's quite old," I said. "But the Chorus is famous."

Back in The Nursery later that night, ready for bed in my red flannel nightshirt, I asked Michael whether he'd had a good time.

"It was a nice evening." He yawned. "But not special the way Christmas dinner was."

"I missed Miss Myra and Miss Mary and talking about the Wales of long ago," I told him. "I actually felt quite nostalgic about it. There's a Welsh word for it—*hiraeth.*"

But on Monday night we would have a poetry reading, and Christmas in Wales would be almost complete. Almost, because there was still one thing I had to do for Mim, if it could be done at all: Find the family.

CHAPTER SEVEN

The Miracle of the Bluestones

This was the day we walked across the spine of the ancient Preseli Hills, a day when Welsh legend came up against scientific fact. And legend won.

Michael and I each dressed in layers of clothing, topped off for me by the duck-hunting jacket and for Michael by his elegant J. Crew coat. I put on Nona's heavy socks and laced up her boots while Michael stepped into his moccasins, still damp from Dinas Island. In the hotel kitchen, we picked up our picnic lunch of leftover turkey sandwiches and a thermos of hot tea.

Michael drove, Nona navigated, and we were off

to the sound of a tape Nona brought, a Welsh harp duo playing Christmas music. Outside, in the yew tree at the edge of the town square, rooks greeted the sunrise with a raucous ovation. We settled into roles that were becoming familiar: Nona was the schoolmistress, full of lore; we were the rapt students.

"Today's walk is described as 'The Mysterious Bluestones of the Preseli Hills,'" Nona began. "Although we call them hills, the word for them in Welsh is *mynydd*—'mountain.' And today we're exploring the area where the famous bluestones of Stonehenge were quarried."

"Why are the bluestones 'mysterious'?" Michael wanted to know.

"You've visited Stonehenge?" Nona asked, and we both nodded. "Well, the great stones of Stonehenge's inner circle are made of bluestones that could not have been quarried anywhere else in the world but at Carnmenyn here in the Preseli Hills! The mystery is how primitive men living almost four thousand years ago could get them all the way from here to the south of England."

"And how did they?" I asked.

"One theory is by water, ferried on rafts down the Irish Sea, then by river to Salisbury Plain. Another theory is by magic. Merlin simply whisked them through the air from the sacred place he knew on the mountain here to the sacred plain there. And I suspect Brian John, the geologist who is leading the walk today, will have his own theory."

"I like the Merlin explanation best," I said, and Nona and I exchanged what Michael calls our "table-tipping" look.

We joined the group of about thirty walkers, men and women ranging in age from two teenage boys to a man in his eighties who was holding a walking stick. Brian John herded us together, introduced himself, and set forth the activities of the day.

"We will walk for almost six hours," he began, "and the pace will be brisk. Please keep together and keep up with the group. I see that some of you are old hands at this game." He glanced approvingly at the battered boots on my feet. "The first walk is to the top of the ridge, up there."

It didn't look steep, but it was. By the time I reached the top thirty minutes later, my cheeks were hot, my heart was pounding, and I was dead last of all the group. Brian John was already speaking. "You are standing on some of the oldest rocks in the world. Pre-Cambrian era, formed more than five hundred million years ago. We know that prehistoric man considered part of these mountains sacred, and we'll see one of those sites this afternoon—the so-called quarry of the bluestones." He nodded in Nona's direction. "I see we have Nona Rees with us today. I'll tell you the geologic reasons for things and ask Nona to fill in the folklore. If you will, Nona?" Nona smiled her agreement.

As we headed toward the rocky outcropping that was our next destination, Brian warned us to walk carefully. The sun was melting the ice underfoot,

the brooks were overflowing from the recent rains, and the ground was slippery
and wet. We crossed a stream. It came
almost to the top of Nona's boots, but not
a drop of water penetrated their tough
hide. Michael was squelching in his moccasins. "Are your feet very wet?" I asked
him.

"Not very," he lied.

Brian waited for us all to catch up. "This is called
Carnarthur, simply 'the place of Arthur.' According to legend, King Arthur stopped here on his way
to a battle. But that's not very likely."

"But Brian," Nona interrupted quietly, "it is *possible,* certainly, since one of his major cities, Caerleon, isn't very far from here. And even *probable;*
given that some of his men held this mountain
sacred, he might have led them here before a battle
to ask the old gods for victory."

Brian scowled. "Oh, Nona, it's possible, but not
scientifically very likely." His tone reminded me of
David Lloyd talking to me on the telephone of
looking for needles in haystacks.

We walked on, and now the group was starting to
string out in ones and twos instead of in the tighter
formation we had managed to keep earlier in the
day. The teenage boys and the old gentleman with
the walking stick were up front with Brian; Nona
and I held the rear. Michael marched ahead of us in
his sodden shoes, looking back every few minutes
to make sure we were okay.

We stopped for lunch at an Iron Age fort. I se-
lected a flat stone to sit on and another to lean
against. It was good to sit after that long walk and
just look out over the moor. The tea had stayed hot
in the thermos, and Nona, Michael, and I passed the
dented metal cup back and forth, sipping slowly so
it would last. My turkey sandwich tasted wonderful. I looked at my watch and was surprised that it
was only one o'clock. Three more hours to go.

On to the next crag. "This is called Beddarthur or
'the tomb of Arthur,'" Brian told us. "It's one of at
least one hundred places in Wales where Arthur is
said to be buried."

Nona spoke up again. "But where would it be
better to bury the High King than these high hills?
High and sacred and old as time?"

Several others in the group were rooting for
Nona's theory, but Brian didn't budge. "Not scientifically probable," he said, and we all walked on.

Finally, toward the end of the walk, we reached
Carnmenyn, "the place of the stones." Brian sat on
one of them, squinted into the sun, and told us

about this place. "The inner circle of Stonehenge is a circle of bluestone megaliths. No question but they came from this mountain, this very spot. Nona, would you give us a few words on Stonehenge?"

"It is the heart of Britain," Nona began. "It was a sacred place before the pyramids were built. According to legend, Merlin raised the ancient 'Giants Dance' as a fitting burial site for his father, Ambrosius the High King. And legend says, too, that as long as the king rests under the stone, the kingdom will not perish." Nona's eyes shone, as they always did when she was recounting wonders. "Stonehenge is a place of mysteries that may never be solved."

"Including the mystery of how those massive stones got from here to there," Brian added. "There are several theories on that, aren't there, Nona?"

Nona recounted the possibilities we had discussed earlier: The stones had been ferried by water or magicked by Merlin.

"And what's *your* theory, Brian?" one of the men asked.

"A perfectly simple one. Glacial ice flow during the Ice Age picked them up here and carried them there. No magic. No miracle."

"Oh, Brian," Nona reproved. "This is a land that believes in miracles. The bluestones went from the most sacred place in all of Wales to the most sacred place in all of England. Isn't that miracle enough?"

For the first time that day, Brian conceded defeat.

He grinned, and his teeth were white against his dark Celtic face. "Miracle enough it is, Nona. Miracle enough."

We started down the ancient mountain. Nona was right, I thought. This country, this Wales of my ancestors, was a place where miracles could still happen.

CHAPTER EIGHT

The Lloyds of Felin Isaf

Jane Writes

I woke up with a feeling of expectation, familiar yet evasive. Then I knew what it was. Every Christmas Eve in Lewisburg, I willed the night to rush by so it would be morning and time to open gifts. The holiday treat at the end of *this* day would be the Lloyds. But could they possibly be the family I wanted to find?

At breakfast, Michael watched me quietly over his coffee cup.

"If it's as important to you as I think it is, we can get a professional to do a real search."

"It *is* important," I told him, "but for now, in the lap of the gods."

We packed, checked out of the Warpool Court, and met Nona in the town square. She handed me a small package. "Belated Christmas gift!" It was an audiotape of the cathedral choir singing Christmas carols.

"We'll play it all year round," Michael said, and we listened to the singing as we drove to Pembroke Castle. It's one of the great Norman castles in Wales, built in the twelfth century by the English invaders to defend themselves against the Welsh. This is a working castle, meant for war, not for romance. Nona showed us the room where Edmund Tudor's young widow, Margaret, not more than fourteen or fifteen years old, gave birth to the future Henry VII, founder of the Tudor dynasty.

"Poor little Margaret," I said, shivering in the freezing room. "She must have been so cold and so alone."

After a pub lunch in Pembroke, we found a shop that sold wine. Michael poked among the bottles, gave a triumphant yelp, and held up his favorite red wine, a California Glen Ellen. Four bottles would be our contribution to dinner.

We drove to the coast and St. Govan's Chapel. It's another of those sacred Welsh places that must have been holy time out of mind. Over centuries, the wind and the sea had eroded the limestone rock into unearthly formations: stalactites and stalagmites, slender stone columns balancing massive boulders, a moonscape of stony rubble.

"Count the stairs leading to the chapel as you go down," Nona suggested. "Then count again going back up. You won't get the same number twice. These are *fairy* stairs that change to keep their secret hidden."

I went carefully down the long flight of stone steps and counted forty-seven. Michael reported thirty-nine. Nona said *she* had stopped counting long since.

The chapel is ancient and simple, with a stone altar, an earthen floor, and a healing well. Nona pointed out a tiny fissure in the rock a few steps from the altar: Govan's original cell. "If you have faith in the saint, you make a wish, stand in the fissure, and—if you can turn around completely inside it—your wish will be granted."

It was a snug fit for me in my baggy hunting coat, but I made a wish to St. Govan and turned solemnly. "You'll get that wish," Nona declared, "as long as you believe he can grant it."

"Oh, I do. I definitely do."

We stood for a while, staring at the rock formations, eerily white against the green sea and the cold blue sky. "I bet I know what you wished," Michael said quietly.

We have been married so long we can read each other's thoughts. "I bet you do, too."

We walked back up the fairy stairs. This time, I counted forty-three; Michael, forty-one. We climbed into our little car, turned on the choir music, and headed for St. David's. The sunset was violent. It lasted for almost an hour, tossing red meteors across the clouds, then turning the whole horizon violet and gold. "If you believe in fairies and St. Govan and medieval romances," I said, "this is a portent."

"Of great good," Nona added. In St. David's, she gave us directions to the old mill, said she would see us at dinner, and left us at the cathedral close.

It was time to meet the Lloyds of Felin Isaf.

Michael Writes

Gail Lloyd must have been watching for our car. She came out into the little courtyard to greet us. "Welcome to Felin Isaf."

We shook hands formally. "*Felin* means 'mill,' doesn't it?" asked Jane, who had been doing her homework.

"'Mill,' it is. *Felin Isaf* actually means 'the lowest mill.' But on our literature for the bed and breakfast, we call it The Old Bishop's Mill to make it a little tonier." Gail helped us carry our luggage inside and we walked through the two-storied central hall, where the great wooden wheel of the mill is on display behind a glass panel. The mill was part of the National Trust, Gail explained. "We not only *wanted* to preserve all of this; we *had* to."

I noted the long table, already set for dinner, a traditional Christmas tree, wreaths of holly, and, on the sideboard, bowls of potpourri that smelled of cloves and cinnamon. "See your room first, get comfortable, then we'll have a sherry before dinner," Gail suggested. We followed her up the steep flight of steps that led to the bedrooms.

Gail Lloyd was an attractive woman in her forties, chestnut-haired, almost as tall as I am. She climbed briskly, carrying our two heaviest bags. A strong woman, I thought.

In our bedroom, Jane oohed over the fresh flowers on the bureau. Gail told us they were periwinkles and winter jasmine from her garden. "Blooming in winter?" Jane asked in surprise.

"It's been an unusual winter," Gail admitted. Beside the vase was a Christmas card from the Lloyd family. "*Croeso i Gymru!*"

Gail showed us how to work the electric teapot and pointed out the suspicious hummocks beneath the down comforter—hot-water bottles to take the chill off the sheets. "I'll put in two hot ones before you go to bed. Now, you settle in. I'll be in the kitchen whenever you're ready to come down."

We were back down quickly, curious to learn more about our host and hostess. We found Gail in the country kitchen, clearly the heart of this house. A big round table filled the center of the room, easy chairs stood about, and books were everywhere, on shelves, on chairs, piled in stacks on the floor. A huge stove, an Aga cooker, took up one entire wall. "That stove is never allowed to go out," Gail said, following my glance.

"It's like my grandmother's stove," Jane said. "I used to be terrified of it because of the red-hot coals beneath the burners, but we always gathered around it on winter mornings when the house was freezing."

There was still no sign of David Lloyd.

We sat and talked while Gail chopped vegetables for the stockpot. She diced carrots, potatoes, celery—peasant vegetables, the vegetables of Miss Mary's cawl soup, the vegetables of winter we had been eating all week in Wales.

"We bought the mill eighteen months ago, thinking the bed-and-breakfast income would help. It has, of course, but not as much as we had hoped. And we spent so much on the restoration!"

"Restorations always cost more than you expect," I told her, adding that I was an architect. "You've done a superb job."

"Thank you," Gail said proudly. "I'm the construction foreman." She told us that she worked part-time at the crafts gallery in town when the bed-

and-breakfast business was slow. As she talked, her hands never stopped chopping, gathering, ordering, which reminded me of the way Jane had described her grandmother's hands when she trimmed a pie-crust.

Welsh men, it seemed, could debate, drink and dream, write poetry and recite it, fight old battles. The Welsh women kept the stoves lighted and the stockpots simmering and told the men how wonderful they were.

Gail told us a little about her husband, carefully, as if she was preparing us. David was brilliant and well educated. "When he set about learning Welsh, he spoke it so elegantly that everyone teased him, and he had to take sandpaper to his accent. And he has a passion for his rugby."

Gail finished chopping and stood up to put the vegetables in the pot. "There's a good bit of anger in him, too. Nona told you we had to sell the Warpool Court?" We nodded. "David is a good man, a good husband and father. He's a bit brusque sometimes." This was said almost as an aside to Jane. "And he's not one for showing his affection. But once he decides you're his kind of people, he will be loyal for life."

The prologue was over. Gail put a lid on the stockpot and led the way into the parlor and the master of Felin Isaf.

David Lloyd had twin barricades in case he needed them—his newspaper and the television set, tuned to sporting news. He shook hands with us gravely, then surveyed Jane. "So this is the American who wants to be our cousin." He would not be easily won over, if won at all.

David poured four glasses of sherry and retreated behind his newspaper again. Gail and Jane discussed her family genealogy, from the Thomas/Lloyd beginnings somewhere here in Carmarthenshire to the coal regions of Pennsylvania.

David Lloyd had been paying attention after all. He peered over his paper and again commented brusquely, "Needle in a haystack."

Gail asked whether we had been enjoying our week in Wales. We told her about Christmas Eve with the carolers and Christmas dinner with the schoolteachers and how welcome we felt.

The newspaper began to descend. "You invited yourselves to Christmas dinner with the teachers?"

"I thought it would be fun for all of us," Jane explained. "And it was."

"Oh, the old dears will live off that story the whole next year. The Americans who could have had Christmas dinner with anybody in St. David's and chose *them*." David poured a second sherry for each of us. He was beginning to thaw.

"Did you see the sunset tonight?" Gail asked. "Wasn't it splendid?"

"It was positively Arthurian," Jane replied.

David looked impressed. "Have you read Malory?"

"My Welsh aunt Mim gave me *Morte d'Arthur* when I was sixteen."

"A good aunt. A good Welsh aunt."

"Yes," Jane said. "She was."

The other dinner guests arrived. Nona, our Nona of the mountaintops, was wearing something positively diaphanous! Gail's sister, Carole, who had been married to David's brother during the years the family ran the Warpool Court, arrived with a scrapbook of family trees she had researched. "All those tiles on the hotel walls, with all those family histories, made me curious. One day, I climbed a ladder and started to study them."

There was one tree, she thought, that would be interesting to Jane. It showed where the Lloyd side of David's family had married the Thomas side. And two of the Thomases had gone to America!

Jane was wide-eyed. Was she going to get her wish? Come on, St. Govan, I urged.

"They went to Pennsylvania?" Jane asked finally.

"No," Carole said. "These two went to Oregon."

Jane's face fell.

Gail served a wonderful dinner, course after course: leek and potato soup, made with leeks grown in her garden, a roasted loin of Welsh pork, carved by David at the sideboard. He impaled the kidney on the carving fork and held it up, gesturing to Jane. "It's a great honor to be singled out for the kidney. Welsh kings were given the kidney as a symbol of their courage. Will you eat it?"

This was a Welsh custom I'd never heard of; the equivalent of getting the sheep's eye at an Arabian banquet? I watched Jane tackle the big kidney gamely, glad that she is an adventurous eater. She got through half of it, so honor was preserved.

There were vegetables and side dishes galore: red

cabbage, brussels sprouts, dressing, gravy, and roast potatoes. We drank the Glen Ellen wine I'd found in Pembroke, then went on to two kinds of pie, apple and mince, a platter of Welsh cheeses, and coffee.

And then, unexpectedly, it was time for the evening's entertainment. David had planned it all, invited friends in to meet us and take part in what he described as "a little eisteddfod." Another Welshman, David Halse, and his pretty, scholarly Irish wife arrived with a bottle of wine to donate to the larder and several books of poetry. We went back to the parlor, gathered around the fireplace, and began the poetry reading. Only the men read. The women listened and applauded.

They read Dylan Thomas, of course.

Now as I was young and easy under the apple boughs
About the lilting house and happy as the grass was green,
The night above the dingle starry,
Time let me hail and climb
Golden in the heydays of his eyes . . .

And then:

Do not go gentle into that good night,
Old age should burn and rave at close of day . . .

Jane was entranced. A Welsh evening of poetry.

Because it was in many ways a family celebration of Christmas, the men read poems about the Nativ-

ity and about faith: More Thomas, T. S. Eliot,
William Blake, Thomas Hardy, John Donne.

It was after midnight. We drank more wine and
David Lloyd sang in a warm baritone, not trained
but true and pleasant: first, Eli Jenkins's prayer
from *Under Milk Wood,* then, in Welsh, "Watching
the White Wheat." "It's a story of lost love. But
then, most Welsh songs are laments for something
lost."

"*Hiraeth,*" Jane suggested.

"*Hiraeth,*" David repeated, looking impressed
again. "And now, what are your special requests, O
guest of honor?"

Jane didn't even need to think. "Shakespeare. A
happy bit of Shakespeare to end the evening. A sonnet."

David Lloyd picked up another volume, turned a
few pages, looked up and began.

> *Let me not to the marriage of true minds*
> *Admit impediments....*

He finished the sonnet. Jane said, "That was
lovely," and started to get up, but David stopped
her. "Oh, no. Oh, no no. You have eaten the kidney; you have the courage of kings. Now it's *your*
turn."

I know what's going on behind Jane's every
expression, and right then, she was suffering a very
rare case of stage fright. She didn't have a poetry
book in her hands, and I knew she wouldn't ask for

one. She was going to do something from memory.

"Well, so far tonight, we haven't heard a word from that other Celt, James Joyce," she said. The room was quiet.

"This is from *Finnegans Wake*. It's the conversation at twilight between the two mythic washerwomen beside the River Liffey, a tale of elm and stone. A night piece that will make us all sleep better." Jane dug somewhere deep down and recited.

Look, look, the dusk is growing! My branches lofty are taking root . . . Can't hear with bawk of bats, all thim liffeying waters of. Ho, talk save us! My foos won't moos. I feel as old as yonder elm. A tale told of Shaun or Shem? All Livia's daughtersons. Dark hawks hear us. Night! Night! My ho head halls. I feel as heavy as yonder stone. Tell me of John or Shaun? Who were Shem and Shaun the living sons or daughters of? Night now! Tell me, tell me, tell me, elm! Night night! Telmetale of stem or stone. Beside the rivering waters of, hitherandthithering waters of. Night!

We all applauded. "Well, it may have been *our* eisteddfod, but *you* are its star," David said. "And who would dare to read another line after you and James Joyce held the floor."

Now it was really time for bed. We joined the Lloyds at the door to say good night to the guests. Jane started up to the bedroom and David said to me, loudly enough for her to hear, "I was proud of Jane tonight. That reading was worthy of a Welshman."

Gail had replaced the hot-water bottles as she had promised and we nestled down into the warmth.

"Why do you think we sleep so well in this country?" Jane asked. "The sleep of innocence?"

"Not in your case," I said sleepily. "In your case, it's the sound of applause."

CHAPTER NINE

Home

We were up early but Gail was already dressed and in the kitchen. The Aga cooker was hot, as always, so would we like a "cooked breakfast"? We said we would happily settle for juice, toast with her home-made jam, and coffee.

"David is coming down. He *never* gets up this early, but there's something important he wants to talk with you about." David entered the kitchen in pajamas and a bathrobe, looking sleepy but resolute.

"You both enjoyed the poetry reading last night?" We agreed we certainly had. "Let's do it again tonight, for your last night in Wales. There's so much we skipped. We didn't read Yeats. Nor *A Child's Christmas in Wales.* You can't leave without *that.*" He was almost pleading.

We told him we would be delighted. Gail said she would try to hunt up a copy of James Joyce somewhere in the house in case Jane wanted to do an encore. David patted Jane's arm. "Don't be too disappointed. We can be your *honorary* relatives."

In the car, I turned on the tape of the St. David's Cathedral choir and listened to Mandy Richardson singing a solo. Jane was pensive. "Last-day blues?" I asked.

"I was really hoping that the Lloyds might turn out to be my cousins. It's crazy, but exactly the kind of craziness Mim loved."

I shook my head. "As Brian John would say, `Not scientifically probable.'"

"But as *Nona* would say," Jane retorted, "this is a country that believes in miracles."

We met Nona at our usual spot and headed for Nevern, where a great Celtic cross stands near the church of St. Brynach.

The churchyard was eerie. Giant yew trees blocked out the sun, so the place was dark and cold, seeming more damned than holy. Nona grabbed Jane by the shoulders and spun her around to face the cross. "There!" she said triumphantly.

"My God." Jane said. "It looks ominous. It's so brooding."

"Like something out of *The Omen*," I agreed.

"Do you know how the Celtic cross came to be?" Nona asked. "The circle was the pagan symbol for the sun, a fertility sign. The early church didn't want all those heathen tributes standing about, so it simply Christianized them by putting a cross within the circle. Voilà! A Celtic cross."

Jane touched the stone cross gingerly. "Maybe the old god doesn't like being displaced and that's why he's brooding."

Nona looked amazed. "I've always thought that," she said, "but you are the only person who has put it into words."

Nona had chosen the Cnapan restaurant for lunch because the food was good *and* it was owned by a family named Lloyd. Mrs. Lloyd—Eluned—came out of the kitchen in her apron to chat with us. Jane explained that she was a Lloyd and a Thomas on her mother's side.

"Then you must meet David and Gail Lloyd of St. David's," Eluned said. "David descends from Lloyds and Thomases, too. Who knows?"

"Not *my* Thomases and Lloyds," Jane said, then explained that we were staying at Felin Isaf. "We compared family trees last night, and David's great-great-grandparents did go to America but not to Pennsylvania, where mine went."

Eluned smiled. "Don't give up hope yet. In Wales, you know, we believe in miracles."

Jane looked the way she does in church during the benediction.

After lunch, we stopped at a bookstore to buy a tape of the harp music Nona had played in the car the previous day. Jane browsed for a while and discovered *A Child's Christmas in Wales*.

Our last sight-seeing stop was the burial chamber of Pentre Ifan. The cromlech, 4,500 years old, is a massive capstone that rests on three stone legs. "We've come full circle," I commented. "Our first

sight in Wales was the birthplace of St. David and
our last is a burial mound."

"No," Jane corrected me. "Our last sight is going
to be David Lloyd reading poetry."

It was time to go home to St. David's for our last
night in Wales.

Jane Writes

David Lloyd ran out of the mill toward us before
we stopped the car. "Hurry!" he called, waving us
inside. "Come see what Gail's found!"

Gail was holding a black book. "I went through
some boxes nobody's opened in years, looking for
the James Joyce. And I found this old, old Bible
from David's family. He didn't even remember having it." It was open to the pages for recording
births, deaths, and marriages.

She squinted at the page. "Does the name Cham-
o-king, Pennsylvania mean anything to you?"

"Cham-o-king?" I whispered. "Could that possibly be Shamokin?"

Gail handed the Bible to me and I squinted at the faded spidery script. There it was. Born in 1885, in the town of Shamokin, Pennsylvania, to David Thomas and Mary Lloyd, a son: Garfield. My great-uncle Garf.

Oh, Mim, I said silently to her, we are home. We are home.

"Well, cousin?" David asked me.

"It's some kind of miracle," I said.

"It is. But don't forget that Wales—"

"Wales is a country that believes in miracles," I said, finishing the sentence for him.

Everybody hugged everybody else, and David poured sherry for a toast to the family. "Welcome home," he said simply, echoing my own thoughts. Dinner passed in a blur of talk as we all exchanged backgrounds and filled in gaps.

Another family member arrived. David had invited his younger brother, Robert, to meet the new relatives from America. Now it was nine o'clock and time for the eisteddfod to begin. Last night's cast gathered again around the fire.

"Somehow we ignored William Butler Yeats last evening," David began. "So, Rob, will you do the honors?"

Rob took the book of poetry and fingered through the pages. "I'll read my favorite."

In a rich Welsh voice that belonged to my uncle Garf, Rob read: "'When you are old and grey and full of sleep . . .'"

We had more Dylan Thomas, more Shakespeare, and more T. S. Eliot. It was almost midnight, and

Gail reminded everyone that Michael and I were leaving at dawn the next day and needed to get some sleep.

"David promised *A Child's Christmas in Wales* tonight," I protested, handing him the little book I'd found that day.

David began.

One Christmas was so much like another, in those years around the sea-town corner now and out of all sound except the distant speaking of the voices I sometimes hear a moment before sleep, that I can never remember whether it snowed for six days and six nights when I was twelve or whether it snowed for twelve days and twelve nights when I was six.

He made the funny parts funnier than I remembered.

For dinner we had turkey and blazing pudding, and after dinner the Uncles sat in front of the fire, loosened all buttons, put their large moist hands over their watch chains, groaned a little and slept.

We laughed, then grew quiet as David read the last lines: the bedtime scene, the end of Christmas Day.

Looking through my bedroom window, out into the moonlight and the unending smoke-coloured snow, I could see the lights in the windows of all the other houses on our hill and hear the music rising from them up the long, steadily falling night. I turned the gas down, I got into bed. I said some words to the close and holy darkness, and then I slept.

The eisteddfod disbanded. Our Christmas in Wales was over.

In our bedroom, Michael was asleep in a moment, but I wasn't quite ready to let this day end. I fussed with the packing and heard the rustle of tissue paper. Suddenly, I remembered why I had brought the angel to Wales—just in case.

Downstairs, the living room was dark except for the tiny lights on the Christmas tree. I took the angel out of the tissue, reached up as high as I could, and placed her on the tree. "You're home, too," I told her.

Back in the bedroom, I took one of Gail's winter jasmine from the vase, shook off a few drops of water, pressed it inside the Dylan Thomas, and heard the distant speaking of voices: Uncle Garf saying grace; Aunt Lib reciting poetry; Gran telling us to drink our cocoa; Mim saying, "Remember me."

I got into bed. I said some words to the close and holy darkness, and then I slept.